CHOICE SHEET

Name_____ Date _____

Preferred basic unit (place a 1 next to your first choice, a 2 next to your second choice, and a 3 next to your third choice).

ROUTIN _____   COPE _____   CRUNODE _____

COMTIN A _____   EMREL _____   DECODE _____

COMTIN B _____   HOPE _____

- -

ASSIGNMENT SHEET

Name _____ Date _____

(The remainder of this form is to be filled out by the coordinator—please leave it blank.)

1. You are the head of the following basic unit: (circle one)

    NONE   ROUTIN   COMTIN A   COMTIN B   HOPE

    COPE   EMREL   CRUNODE   DECODE

2. You are controller of the following function: (circle one)

    None   Base Wages   Communication Tickets

3. You are assigned to the following division: (circle one)

    Red   Yellow   Blue   Green

_____
(Note: These forms must be presented to the coordinator for someone to play The Organization Game.)

THE ORGANIZATION GAME

A SIMULATION

PARTICIPANT'S MANUAL

THIRD EDITION

ROBERT H. MILES
School of Business
Emory University

W. ALAN RANDOLPH
Merrick School of Business
University of Baltimore

EDWARD R. KEMERY
Merrick School of Business
University of Baltimore

HarperCollins*CollegePublishers*

Dedicated to Our Students

Please note: Forms A and B on page i must be present for someone to play The Organization Game.

Participant's Manual to accompany Miles/Randolph/Kemery THE ORGANIZATION GAME: A SIMULATION, Third Edition

ISBN: 0-673-46861-5

93 94 95 96 97   9 8 7 6 5 4 3 2 1

CONTENTS

Forms A and B
(Choice Sheet and Assignment Sheet)

Preface

Instructor's Note

PART ONE
THE ORGANIZATION GAME   1

Introduction   2

Coordinator's Role   2

Nature of the Rules   3

Summary of the Rules   4

  Orgdollars   4

  Divisions   4

  Division Transfers   4

  Inter-division Communications   4

  Personnel Expenses   5

  Basic Operating Units   5

  Unit Heads   5

  Absenteeism   6

  Task Assignments   6

  Dismissals and Quits   6

  Base Wage   6

  Permanently Idle and Temporarily Idle   6

  Options   7

  Individual Goals   7

  Performance Indicators   7

  Management Function   7

  Strikes   7

  Special Events   8

  Objectives of the Simulation   8

Orgdollars *8*
    Players' Envelopes 9

Divisions *9*
    Transfers 9

Inter-division Communications *10*
    Communication Ticket 10
    Permanent Communication Certificate 10
    Communication Ticket Controller 11
    Restrictions on Inter-division Communications 11

Personnel Expenses *11*

Basic Operating Units *13*
    Early Tasks of the Operating Units 13
    Types of Units 13

ROUTIN *14*
    Overall Objective 14
    What ROUTIN Does 14
    Effects of ROUTIN on Performance Indicators 15
    Suggested Roles in ROUTIN 16

COMTIN A and B *16*
    Overall Objective 16
    The Two Sub-units of COMTIN 16
    What COMTIN Does 16
    Effects on Organizational Performance Indicators 18
    Suggested Roles in COMTIN Sub-units 18

CRUNODE *19*
    Overall Objective 19
    What CRUNODE Does 19
    Suggested Roles in CRUNODE 20
    Income Budgeted for Each Performance Session 20

EMREL *20*
    Overall Objective 20
    What EMREL Does 20
    Suggested Roles in EMREL 22

Income Budgeted for Each Performance
Session 22

DECODE 23

Overall Objective 23

What DECODE Does 23

Suggested Roles in DECODE 23

Income Budgeted for Each Performance
Session 24

COPE 24

Overall Objective 24

What COPE Does 24

Suggested Roles in COPE 25

Income Budgeted for Each Performance
Session 25

HOPE 25

Overall Objective 25

What HOPE Does 25

Suggested Roles in HOPE 26

Income Budgeted for Each Performance
Session 26

Unit Heads 26

Powers of Unit Heads 26

Replacing Unit Heads 27

Stating Your Preferences 27

Absenteeism 28

Task Assignments 29

Dismissals and Quits 30

Base Wages 30

Permanent Base Wage Certificate 31

Base Wage Controller 31

Failure to Provide Base Wage 31

Repeated Base Wage Failure 32

Permanently Idle and Temporarily Idle   32

Options   33
    E-mail Option   33
    Vacation Option   33
    Communication Ticket Purchase Option   34
    Job Protection Ticket Option   34
    Highest Savings Award Option   34
    Compensation Plan Option   34
    Other Options   34

Individual Goals   35

Performance Indicators   36
    Reinvestment in Organization   37
    Changes in the Performance Indicators   38
    Consequences of Different Values of
        Performance Indicators   40

Management Function   41

Strikes   41
    Initiating a Strike   41
    Resolution of Grievances   42
    Dues and Fines   43
    Terminating a Strike   43

Special Events (Optional)   44

Summary   44

PART TWO
PLAYERS' FORMS   47

List of Players' Forms   49
    Form C   Division Transfer Sheet   51
    Form D   Permanent Communication Certificate   51
    Form E   Permanent Base Wage Certificate   51
    Form F   Transfer of Certificates or
                Controllerships   53
    Form G   Unit Task Assignment Schedule   55

Form H   ROUTIN Task Unit: Input-Output
Form   61

Form I   Withdrawal/Deposit of Assets Form   65

Form J   DECODE Organizational
Diagnosis Report   67

Form K   COMTIN Task Unit: Input-Output
Form   71

Form L   Declaring a Strike   77

Form M   Strike Termination Form   79

Form N   Assessment Form   81

Form O   Dismissal Form   85

Form P   Quit Form   85

Form Q   Vacation Form   89

Form R1   Investment Form   91

Form R2   HRD Investment Form   93

Form R3   HRD Investment Report Form   95

Form S   EMREL Base Wage Report Form   97

Form T   EMREL Task Assignment Status
Report   101

Form U   COPE Report of Financial Operations   105

Form V   CRUNODE Information Report   109

Form W   Job Protection Ticket   113

Form X   Savings Award Form   115

PREFACE

The Organization Game was developed to provide a realistic setting in which individuals can experience managing an organization in complex, dynamic times, such as we find today. It allows participants to experiment with key concepts and issues in the management of organizations, organizational behavior, organization theory, and organization change. The challenge of the simulation is for participants to integrate and apply their knowledge and skills related to individual, interpersonal, group, inter-group, and organizational behaviors to the design and management of their simulated organization. In so doing they must deal with diversity, international concerns, quality issues, and a variety of other organizational issues.

Participants in *The Organization Game* can succeed or fail. This manual outlines the differentiated operating units and divisions and the basic ground rules of the simulation. Participants in *The Game* actively create an organization, elaborate its rationalization and institutionalization, and develop the mechanisms for adapting to the internal and external forces of change and complexity.

As with all simulations, trade-offs had to be made between operational reality and feasibility. Practitioners and students who have participated in earlier versions of the simulation over the past fifteen years have told us that *The Game* is a realistic simulation of life in a complex, dynamic organization. Of course, what a participant derives from any simulation depends in large measure on the effort he or she devotes to the experience.

So, *get involved!* If you do not receive an initial task assignment, work vigorously to obtain one. Failing that, invent your own! *Be creative!*

Before discussing the general rules and basic structure of *The Game*, we must acknowledge our intellectual debt to William A. Gamson, a pioneer in behaviorally played simulations. His *SIMSOC: Simulated Society* was a rich source from which to draw in developing the present simulation of life in a complex organization.

We owe a special debt of gratitude to the many students, professionals, and managers who have participated in previous versions of *The Game*. They participated fully, and the recommendations they made both during and after play were the bases upon which this revised version of *The Organization Game* was built. These participants represented not only our own institutions but also a variety of public- and private-sector organizations, including small and large business firms producing a wide range of goods and services, banks, insurance companies, instrumentalities of federal, state, and municipal government, educational institutions, hospitals, public welfare and mental health agencies, and the armed services.

Special thanks are also owed to a number of individuals who used *The Organization Game* and provided suggestions for revising this and earlier editions. In particular, Barry Posner, Santa Clara University, and David Rikert, Nike, Inc., have been and continue to be most helpful in offering suggestions and new special events (several in this edition are credited to them). In addition, the following individuals made very helpful suggestions regarding *The Game:* Kim Cameron, University of Michigan; David Whetten, University of Illinois; Diane Ferry, University of Delaware; Lauke Parke, University of Vermont; Jim Cashman, University of Alabama; Joe Selzer, Lasalle University; Len Schlesinger, Harvard Business School; Randall Sleeth, Virginia Commonwealth University; Bill Torbert, Boston College; and Peter Frost, University of British Columbia.

Without the help of these individuals, *The Game* would not have reached its current level of sophistication. Their sustained interest in this endeavor convinces us that we will continue to depend on the advice we receive from future users of and participants in *The Organization Game* to assure its refinement and evolution.

Finally, we also express our sincere appreciation to our two universities for providing the atmosphere that has encouraged innovation in our teaching.

R. H. M.   W. A. R.   E. R. K.
Atlanta, GA   Baltimore, MD Baltimore, MD

INSTRUCTOR'S NOTE

To play *The Organization Game*, each participant must have a copy of the *Participant's Manual*, complete with all players' forms. Forms A and B at the front of this manual are essential to playing *The Game*. To emphasize the importance of these forms, players who do not have them are usually penalized. In addition, each instructor needs an *Administrator's Guide*, which contains instructions and materials for running the simulated organization. One *Guide* is needed for each simulation. Additional copies can be obtained from HarperCollins College Publishers, 10 East 53rd Street, New York, NY 10022.

The Organization Game is behaviorally played and manually or computer scored. It does not rely on computers or other mechanical devices though they can be used to enhance *The Game*, as explained in the *Administrator's Guide*. Experienced users of *The Game* may find helpful a summary of the changes that have been made for this third edition in the *Administrator's Guide* on pages 57-58.

Part One

The Organization Game

Introduction

Very soon you will be participating in *The Organization Game* as a member of a simulated organization, dealing with production and cost issues, quality concerns, diversity and international concerns, and a variety of team and organizational issues. As you prepare to play, you will discover that many rules and forms must be relied upon to simulate the complexity of a real organization. Each rule has a specific purpose in terms of making the simulation realistic. There are too many tasks for one person to perform and too many rules for any individual player to comprehend and memorize totally. To master this complexity, and the dynamism of the simulation, you will need organization processes, management, and leadership.

If the simulation is to be a valuable learning experience, the coordinator will need your cooperation. Cooperation in this context means taking seriously your participation in the organizing and managing processes inherent in the simulation.

Some of the goals you bring to *The Game* or develop during your participation will be the same as those of other participants; in fact, the achievement of your goals will depend in part on the efforts of others in your organization. Some of your goals will also bring you into conflict with others. Inevitably, some of you will do better than others in achieving your goals.

Initially you are all members of the organization. The external environment of the simulated organization (e.g., other organizations, regulatory bodies, and their members and representatives) will exist only in imaginary form. Certain ground rules of the game are based on assumptions about the reactions of these imaginary forces in your organization's internal and external environments. You will discover, however, that the restrictions on game play owing to these assumptions are minimal. Respecting these rules will still provide considerable freedom for you to design and change the organization and its parts so that individual, group, or organizational objectives may be achieved.

Experience has shown that what you get out of *The Organization Game* is a direct function of the amount of thought and energy you devote to it during play. For those who have invested themselves as active participants, *The Game* has become a worthwhile, enduring, and fond memory of their struggle to understand the management of organizations and the attitudes, behaviors, and experiences of their members.

Coordinator's Role

The coordinator's role is kept to an absolute minimum once the organization is in process. The coordinator is not a part of your organization. He or she is part of your environment and will maintain the resource pool, receive forms, and carry out other duties specified in the manual to make the game operate. He or she will not perform actions that will arbitrarily make the game more difficult.

Furthermore, if questions about the rules arise after the organization is in progress, the coordinator will only refer you to the manual. *He or she will not interpret the rules for you, nor will he or she advise you on how to deal with situations that arise in the game.* The coordinator's knowledge about the game is limited by the rules in the manual, and any issues not covered by the manual can be defined in any way the organization sees fit. Finally, the coordinator normally will not announce in advance when the game will end. This precaution is necessary to avoid "end-of-game" artifacts that might otherwise influence organizational behaviors and outcomes. In short, the coordinator will do everything to avoid becoming enmeshed as a participant in your organization once it has begun.

Nature of the Rules

The rules in the manual are intended to represent certain parameters within which your simulated organization must exist. The rules are not alterable by either your fellow members or the coordinator. To ignore them by neglect or intent simply renders the game pointless; they represent a minimal foundation upon which your organization may be built. The coordinator should not be put in the position of having to monitor your observance of the rules but should be able to depend on your cooperation to achieve the larger purpose of learning about organizations. If you willfully break the rules, the coordinator will have no choice but to impose fines on the organization.

As you will see, the rules of the manual allow great leeway for you to add your own agreements and rules. The agreements that you make among yourselves are your own responsibility to enforce. They may represent individual pacts or internal policies set by the organization or its units. If a player ignores or refuses to comply with a policy or rule that your organization makes, you must face the issue of how to deal with this behavior. All players have a responsibility to observe the rules in the manual to make the game work, but they have no such responsibility toward rules that you may establish for yourselves.

In spite of efforts to anticipate various contingencies, ambiguous situations will inevitably arise. The coordinator will not interpret such ambiguities but will refer the question back to the organization for interpretation. The coordinator will be concerned only with those aspects of the ambiguous situation that affect his or her tasks.

A final note about the manual and the rules is that they provide only a minimal basis for the game in terms of tasks to be performed in the organization. *Be creative* in determining the needs of your organization and in accomplishing tasks that need to be performed to make your organization succeed.

Summary of the Rules

The rules that follow this introductory section are detailed, and understanding them will require some teamwork among organizational members. In an effort to reduce some of the initial uncertainty you may experience, a short summary of the rules follows to give you a general sense of the nature of the organization and the constraints and options with which you must operate. This summary also includes page references so that you can easily look up necessary details. A careful reading of this summary is a helpful way to begin, *but you must read and re-read* the complete rules if you are to play *The Organization Game* effectively. Once play has begun, you will find yourself using this manual as a decision-making tool and a guide to action, so attempt to develop a feel for where the answers are to questions which may arise during play.

Orgdollars

Orgdollars (Org$) serve as the basic currency for your simulated organization. Initially, Org$ are held by the coordinator in the common resource pool. Various amounts are distributed to designated members at the beginning of each period of play based on rules specified in the manual (pp. 8-9).

Divisions

Each member of the organization is at all times assigned to one of four major divisions of the simulated organization (p. 9).

Division Transfers

A player may move to another division of the organization by paying a transfer expense to the coordinator or by receiving a primary task assignment in a unit of another division (pp. 9-10).

Interdivision Communications

A member may not communicate between divisions unless he or she has either a **Communication Ticket** or a **Permanent Communication Certificate**. Communication tickets may be obtained from a limited number of members who are controllers and receive a predetermined supply of tickets each session. The number of tickets given each controller is fixed, but the number of controllers depends on the size of your organization. A permanent communication certificate may be purchased coordinator. Possession of either a ticket or certificate permits the bearer to go to another division in the organization to communicate with members of that division (pp. 10-11).

Personnel Expenses

At the beginning of the simulation all participants are considered employees of the simulated organization, but only unit heads and controllers have formal task assignments. There are expenses associated with assigning other members to perform other tasks. Each employee must receive a **Base Wage Ticket** each session and may negotiate for other wages and benefits when assigned a task. Should a unit decide to dismiss a member, a dismissal expense must be paid to the coordinator (pp. 11-12).

Basic Operating Units

Your simulated organization has eight basic operating units in which you may find a task assignment. Quality and cost effectiveness are prime concerns of all eight units. The units are distributed across the four divisions in a manner prescribed by *The Game* instructions. Only the heads of these units will be designated by the coordinator at the beginning. The rest of the unit's work force must come from members who have no initial task assignment. At the beginning of each session, the head of each unit receives the unit's income to dispense.

There are three producing units (ROUTIN and COMTIN A and B), an employee relations unit (EMREL), an information-processing and information-dissemination unit (CRUNODE), an internal management consulting unit (DECODE), an internal audit unit (COPE), and a coalition or interest group (HOPE). You should read the descriptions of these units before beginning play, because you will be asked to designate three choices among them (p. 27-28), and if you are not picked as head of a unit, you will be faced with finding a task to perform within one of the basic units (pp. 13-14).

Controller functions are not considered assigned to one of the seven basic operating units but rather to one of the four divisions. Persons performing these functions are regarded as having a formal task assignment, but they may not employ others.

Unit Heads

Unit heads are responsible for providing leadership with regard to effectiveness, diversity, and quality. They are responsible for assigning members to and dismissing members from their units, are the recipients of the unit's income, and have primary responsibility for achieving the unit's goals. It is possible for the unit head to be voluntarily or involuntarily removed (pp. 26-28).

Absenteeism

Certain performance indicators are lowered when members are absent, regardless of reason (p. 28).

Task Assignments

A member may be formally assigned only one task at a time (Form G). The member is automatically assigned to the division containing his or her assigned task unit, unless the Division Transfer Sheet (Form C) is processed. For each member assigned to a new task, certain of the performance indicators are affected, some positively and some negatively. Also, the unit must pay an expense to the coordinator for each individual assigned or dismissed. A member may perform tasks for an operating unit on terms he or she negotiates with the unit head; but regardless of the details of the task assignment agreement, the unit must provide a base subsistence wage ticket for each of its members. All task assignments must be processed through EMREL (p. 29-30).

Dismissals and Quits

For each person who is dismissed from or who quits his or her task in an operating unit, all performance indicators are lowered for the period in which the action occurs. Also, the member will be immediately transferred to the Red Division. If the unit dismisses an employee, that unit must bear the expense incurred (pp. 30).

Base Wages

In order to remain a viable member of the organization, each player must obtain and present to the coordinator through EMREL a base wage ticket for each performance session. Members may obtain this base wage ticket in many ways, but units listing members as task assignees on the Unit Task Assignment Schedule (Form G) must at least pay them a base wage ticket. The organization should ensure that each of its members receives at least a base wage ticket (pp. 30-32).

Permanently Idle and Temporarily Idle

Failure to obtain and present a base wage ticket to the coordinator for an organization member before the end of each period results initially in the member being classified as "temporarily idle" and finally as "permanently idle." Both categories result in declines in the performance indicators, and a permanently idle status results in removal of the member from play (pp. 32-33).

Options

The coordinator will announce any options that may be available (pp. 33-34). For example, one option makes it possible for members to take vacations. Another option makes it possible to communicate between divisions using e-mail.

Individual Goals

It is recommended that all players have personal as well as group and organizational goals to make the simulation more realistic (pp. 35).

Performance Indicators

Numerical values for four organizational performance indicators are calculated at the end of each period of play. The indicators are **Resource Base, Total Output, Internal Cohesion,** and **Member Commitment.** These indicators may be raised by investing Org$ in either of two programs: Organizational Improvement and Human Resources Development. The indicators can also be raised by effective generation of the organization's output (the tasks of ROUTIN and COMTIN A and B).

The performance indicators automatically decline by a certain percentage each period and can be lowered further by various actions and events that occur in the organization's life. If the indicators decline below certain points, the income available to the basic units in the organization declines, and if the indicators rise above a certain point, the income available to the basic units increases. If any performance indicator falls below zero, the organization has failed and the simulation is over (pp. 36-41).

Management Function

There is no requirement that the members establish a management structure or formal rules and policies for regulating such a structure (p. 41). However, the members must determine ways to effectively manage the organization and all matters the organization confronts.

Strikes

Any individual or group of individuals may create a *strike* with the power to withhold their work and demand a hearing of their concerns. The members of a strike are protected from dismissal while the strike is in effect. If a grievance cannot be resolved during the strike, the strike can be renewed.

It is possible for a strike to be canceled before it would automatically expire, and if the strike involves work stoppage, there are still means for the organization to accomplish its tasks. Strikes have adverse effects on the performance indicators to the extent that work stoppage is involved (pp. 41-44).

Special Events

The coordinator may announce the occurrence of certain external events that can affect the organization's operations. Special events focus on environmental change and international issues, among other matters. You will not be informed in advance when they will occur (if at all) or what their nature will be (p. 44).

Objectives of the Simulation

Your objectives should be to achieve your personal goals, to help your unit achieve its goals, and to help your organization be a success. If you try to achieve these goals, the larger objective of learning about organizations will be achieved (p. 44).

Orgdollars

Orgdollars (Org$) are the basic monetary units in your simulated organization. You may use them to purchase things you require to achieve your individual, group, and organizational goals. For example, Org$ may be used to purchase resources needed to accomplish the primary organizational tasks or to acquire the ability to communicate across major organizational divisions. You may also use Org$ to make investments in organizational programs and to employ others, or you may decide to save them for use in a future session. Like money in the real world, the uses to which you put your Org$ are largely up to you. As you read this manual, you will discover the many ways in which you may use Org$.

The coordinator will maintain all Org$ not owned by an individual or unit in the organization. The coordinator will handle deposits and withdrawals of assets of the basic task units. The coordinator will also distribute earned income to the basic operating units at the beginning of each session at a rate specified in this manual (pp. 14-26). The coordinator does not normally make loans or extend credit.

Players' Envelopes

Each player is assumed to have a secure place to keep Org$ and all other relevant papers and forms. This secure place is represented by an envelope distributed to each player by the coordinator at the beginning of the first session of play.

At the end of each session, all envelopes *must be delivered* to the coordinator, who will place appropriate materials (e.g., earned income, messages, etc.) in them for the next session. It is your responsibility to see that the coordinator gets your envelope at the end of each session. The coordinator will not inspect the contents of the envelopes. So, *do not place anything in the envelope that you wish to deliver to the coordinator.* Furthermore, the coordinator will not remove anything from the envelopes. Anything you wish the coordinator to receive must be given to him or her before the end of the session.

It is against the rules for a player to take Org$ or other items from another player's envelope. The same rule applies to the Org$ and other materials (e.g., tickets, certificates, forms, etc.) held by the coordinator. Counterfeiting and forgery are also strictly prohibited by the rules of the game, and penalties can apply if members are caught counterfeiting Org$.

Each envelope should bear the player's preferred first name and last name, assigned division, and unit (only if head).

Divisions

At the beginning of the simulation each participant is assigned to one of the four divisions of the simulated organization. These divisions are designated as Red, Yellow, Blue, and Green. At all times, players have a division identification, but it is possible for players to transfer from one division to another and to communicate with members of other divisions. *Players must return to their assigned divisions at the end of each session.*

Transfers

A player is automatically transferred to the division containing the task unit to which he or she is initially assigned or reassigned after dismissal, quitting, or inadvertent loss of job (e.g., failure to turn in a base wage ticket). The task assignment expense covers any necessary transfer fee. Any other transfer of a player from one division to another must be initiated by filing Form C with the coordinator and paying a $5 transfer expense. The transfer does not become effective until the beginning of the period following the filing of this form and payment.

Transfers are subject to the following restrictions. First, no more than one-third of the total organizational membership (including absentees) may be assigned to any one division. Second, a player cannot transfer without the majority consent of the unit heads in the two divisions involved in the transfer.

The basic operating units and the controller functions (communications and base wages) are permanently domiciled in their divisions of origin. They may not be transferred from one division to another and *their primary tasks must be performed in their assigned divisions*. This rule simulates one of the constraints created by the nature of the technologies used by the various units.

Interdivision Communications

Although there are no restrictions on communications among members within a division, moving from division to division to engage in face-to-face, interdivision communications requires the possession of either a communication ticket or a permanent communication certificate. *No one* may engage in face-to-face communications between divisions unless he or she possesses either a communication ticket or a permanent communication certificate.

Communication Ticket

A person who possesses a communication ticket may use it to go to other divisions. A communication ticket is good for one trip only (a trip is defined as leaving and returning to the assigned division with no more than one stop in each other division). *It is the player's responsibility to give the coordinator or an assistant his or her communication ticket at the beginning of each trip.* Ticket privileges expire upon return to the division of assignment. Communication tickets may be obtained from members who are Communication Ticket Controllers, as discussed below.

Permanent Communication Certificate

For those who desire more flexible alternatives for interdivision communication, Permanent Communication Certificates are available. For a cost of $25, delivered along with a completed Form D to the coordinator, you may obtain a permanent communication certificate. This certificate entitles its holders to unlimited communication rounds between the divisions throughout the remaining play.

Only the person purchasing the certificate is entitled to use it, except that it may be transferred to another player by filing Form F with the coordinator along with a transfer expense of $3.

Communication Ticket Controllers

A limited number of players will be designated as Communication Ticket Controllers during the initial assignments in *The Game*. The number of controllers depends on the size of the organization, which the coordinator announces at the beginning of play. These controllers will each receive five communication tickets per session, which they can use, hoard, dispense, save, or sell in any fashion they see fit. Unused tickets may be carried over to future sessions; in addition, the duties of the controller, as well as the session's supply of five communication tickets, may be transferred to another person, but a $3 transfer charge must be given to the coordinator along with a completed Form F. If a player performing the role of the controller is absent for any reason, his or her supply of communication tickets for that session is lost to the organization. Communication Ticket Controllers are considered to have a formal task assignment, but they may not employ others. Since controllers are considered task assigned, no hiring fee is needed for them, but their names must appear on Forms S and T. Also, they must receive a base wage ticket for each session, or they lose their position as controllers and are sent to the Red Division, and the organization loses the 5 communication tickets per session until a new controller is appointed. Finally, the controller must remain within his or her original division.

Restrictions on Interdivision Communications

1. No more than half of the total number of participants in the organization may be present in one division at the same time.
2. Communication is normally permitted only within the four divisions. Communication between players is, for example, prohibited in the halls, around the coordinator's station, and on breaks. The only exception is if you pay the coordinator $10 per person to be able to meet off site (facilities permitting).
3. Any player may be refused admission to a division by unanimous consent of the members assigned to that division.

Personnel Expenses

At the beginning of the simulation, everyone except the heads of the basic operating units and the controllers must find a task assignment in one of the operating units. Thus, there are personnel placement activities that must be performed and that have associated costs.

The members in the various divisions who remain unassigned and do not receive a base wage ticket have a substantial negative effect on the performance indicators (see Table 3, p. 42). Assigning people to jobs (task assignment) has both a negative and a positive effect in the short run and creates an expense for the organization, which is borne at the unit level. The long-run effect, however, is positive as long as the people assigned do not quit, are not dismissed, and do not lose their task through failure to obtain a base wage.

All assignments must be accomplished by submitting the Unit Task Assignment Schedule (Form G) and $5 per new assignee through EMREL to the coordinator. Form G and the $5 apply to initial job assignments, reassignments, and new assignments after dismissals, quits, and job loss from base wage failure. All dismissals must likewise be accomplished by submitting Form O and a dismissal expense of $5 through EMREL to the coordinator. *All task assignments and dismissals, with appropriate fees, must be routed through EMREL to the coordinator.* EMREL maintains a master task assignment schedule and a base wage report (Forms S and T). EMREL is obliged to forward all transactions and fees to the coordinator in exactly the manner specified by the unit head.

When a member quits, Form R must be filed with the coordinator; no fee is required. All employees listed on a Unit Task Assignment Schedule (Form G) must receive a base wage ticket (or the equivalent base wage certificate) from the unit for each period in which they are assigned. It is the unit head's responsibility to ensure that this minimal base wage obligation is honored, and this is represented by routing a base wage ticket through EMREL to the coordinator or providing the person with a permanent base wage certificate. Other compensation in Org$ or fringe benefits of the task agreement are worked out by the unit head and assignee, sometimes in conjunction with EMREL or some other third party, and are not the concern of the coordinator. However, the organization may decide to develop a compensation scheme that allows for payment above the base wage level.

Other expenses associated with personnel are transfer expenses (Form C and $5) for moving a member from one division to another (though it is not necessary that a member be assigned to the same division as his or her task unit) and, sometimes, interdivision communication expenses. Also, EMREL may decide to charge for its services; so may other individuals or groups within the organization. Only the expenses represented by forms submitted to the coordinator are monitored and enforced by the coordinator.

Finally, some provision must be made to provide base wage tickets or permanent base wage certificates to members who do not have a formal task assignment. These members are regarded as underutilized, and this status may result in permanent idleness within the organization if they become chronically neglected by the members of active organizational units.

Basic Operating Units

Before the organization begins, you will be asked to express your first, second, and third preferences for the role of unit head in one of the eight basic operating units described below. (Forms A and B are for this purpose.) These preferences will be used only in selecting the head of each unit. Other unit members must be added as needed by the following task assignment procedure.

Early Tasks of the Operating Units

When *The Game* begins, one of the first tasks will be for heads of the basic units to staff and organize their units. This initial staffing and organizing phase is accomplished when a Unit Task Assignment Schedule (Form G) is forwarded from each unit head, through EMREL, to the coordinator. Except for unit heads and controllers, no one is considered assigned to an operating unit until the coordinator receives these schedules in proper form and with the appropriate fees.

EMREL is responsible for maintaining a master Base Wage Report and Task Assignment Status Report (Forms S and T). EMREL is obliged by the rules of the simulation to serve as the agent of the unit heads on matters of task assignments, dismissals, and base wage accounting. EMREL will submit a master Task Assignment Status Report and a Base Wage Report, with appropriate fees and wage certificates, to the coordinator before the end of each session.

In the pages that immediately follow, each of the operating units is described in some detail. These descriptions contain various roles that might be helpful in staffing the unit, but they are suggestive only. If you have other ideas for unit jobs, feel free to use them. Remember, there are no tricks in the way the game is set up: The coordinator will only do what the manual requires.

Types of Units

There are two basic types of units: production units and support units. Production units carry out the tasks of making the products of the organization. Support units are needed to support these operations and to take care of things that the production units are not equipped to handle.

Production units receive a portion of their return on operations in the form of income (10% of assets per session), and support units receive a stipulated budget per session (both adjusted depending on the values of the performance indicators; see p. 38-41). For each unit, two different budget figures are displayed in the description of the unit: Size One and Size Two. This means that the budget of a unit depends on the size (number of members) of the organization. This size will be announced by the coordinator prior to the beginning of play and will not change over the life of the organization. Thus, you should keep in mind the size of the organization in making decisions about its management. A description of each of the basic operating units follows.

ROUTIN (pronounced "rū'-tĭn")

Overall Objective

To produce quality words and expand the return on its operations as much as possible.

What ROUTIN Does

ROUTIN, located in the Yellow Division, produces words from anagrams—combinations of letters in jumbled order. This task must be performed in the Yellow Division. ROUTIN's resources (assets) and return (income) may be increased by the operations described below.

In each period of play, ROUTIN can purchase anagrams from the coordinator using Form H, but the capacity of the technology limits the number of anagrams that are available at any time. Therefore, ROUTIN may purchase only up to 10 anagrams during a given session, and these anagrams need not all be purchased at the same time. All anagrams purchased must be authorized by the head of ROUTIN, using Form H, and there is a $5 charge for placing each order.

The cost of each anagram depends on the size of the organization and is given in Table 1. An anagram is solved by using its letters to complete a six-letter word found in any standard dictionary (proper names excluded). Use of a dictionary to solve anagrams is, however, strictly prohibited by the rules of *The Organization Game*. Quality and cost effectiveness are primary concerns of ROUTIN.

Completed words must be submitted to the coordinator on Form H *before the end of the session in which they were purchased. Credit for completed words is not received until the beginning of the next period of play.* For each completed word, ROUTIN resources (assets), which are maintained by the coordinator, will be increased in accordance with Table 1. Essentially, ROUTIN will receive for each completed word 250% of the cost of the anagram, and this money will be added to their asset account.

The anagrams that ROUTIN buys will vary in difficulty, but there will be on average four chances in ten of buying an anagram that has no solution. This does not necessarily mean that, in any given period, you will be able to solve exactly six out of ten anagrams. It might be that in some periods you will be able to solve all anagrams purchased, and in others, only one or two anagrams: but in the long run about 60% will be solvable. The coordinator will sell anagrams in a predetermined, random order over which he or she has no control.

The head of ROUTIN can withdraw part or all of its resources (assets) from the asset account maintained by the coordinator whenever he or she wishes by filling out and signing Form I and presenting it to the coordinator. Also, Form I can be used to deposit Org$ in ROUTIN's asset pool. These assets as well as the income they generate (10% each session or as adjusted, depending on the values of the performance indicators; see pp. 38-41) may be used to buy anagrams, make investments in programs, purchase tickets and certificates, attract members to perform ROUTIN tasks, and so forth.

At the beginning, however, ROUTIN assets and income are not enough to purchase 10 anagrams. To purchase 10 anagrams, ROUTIN must negotiate additional Org$ from other parts of the organization, using whatever means and promises it deems appropriate.

Any task assignments made by the head of ROUTIN must be formalized by submitting a Unit Task Assignment Schedule (Form G), or revision thereof, with appropriate fees, through EMREL to the coordinator. Base wage tickets as well as dismissal forms should also be handled through EMREL.

Effects of ROUTIN on Performance Indicators

Anagram purchases and completions affect three of the performance indicators (described more fully on pp. 36-41), but in different ways. For each anagram purchased, the Resource Base indicator of the organization is reduced, but for each completed anagram both Total Output and Member Commitment indicators are increased. Thus, the completion of ROUTIN tasks has both short-term costs and longer-term benefits for the organization.

TABLE 1	Summary of ROUTIN Assets, Income, Costs, and Payoffs[a] (in Org$)			
Size	Starting Assets	Income in First Session[b]	Cost per Anagram	Increase in Assets for Completed Word
One	100	10	20	50
Two	150	15	30	75

[a] Probability of buying an unsolvable anagram = 40%.
[b] Thereafter ROUTIN receives 10% (or as adjusted depending on the values of the performance indicators—see pp. 34-35) of its assets distributed to the unit head at the beginning of each session.

Suggested Roles in ROUTIN

1. *Chief Accountant:* Someone responsible for managing ROUTIN'S funds.
2. *Work Team Leader:* Someone responsible for the efforts directed at word completion from anagrams.
3. *Quality Analyst:* Someone responsible for tracking and evaluating the effectiveness of ROUTIN task operations.
4. *Worker:* Someone responsible for doing the work on anagrams.
5. Other roles as deemed appropriate. *Be creative.*

COMTIN A and B (pronounced "cŏm'-tǐn")

Overall Objective

To solve complex word problems and expand the return on their operations as much as possible.

The Two Sub-units of COMTIN

COMTIN is made up of two sub-units, each having its own head. Sub-unit A of COMTIN and its head are located in the Green Division. Sub-unit B of COMTIN and its head are located in the Yellow Division. The mission of COMTIN requires the efforts of both sub-units, and each sub-unit must perform its task in its assigned division.

What COMTIN Does

COMTIN develops words from puzzles. Its resources (assets) and return (income) may be increased by providing this service through the following operations.

In each period of play, either or both sub-units of COMTIN may acquire blank word puzzles from the coordinator, but the supply of these puzzles is limited by the technology to five in any one session. Not all puzzles need to be acquired at the same time; however, a charge of $5 must be paid to process each puzzle order. This charge must be paid to the coordinator and accompanied by Form K, which must have been completed and signed by the head of either COMTIN A or B.

Thus, either the head of COMTIN A or B may initiate a request for word puzzles using Form K. *However, once an order has been processed by the coordinator, half of each word puzzle must be picked up by Sub-unit A, and the other half must be picked up by Sub-unit B.* Both sub-units must work on their half of the puzzle in their respective divisions. Credit for a completed puzzle will be granted only if the original Form K with solved puzzle(s) is received by the coordinator prior to the end of the session in which it was initiated. A completed puzzle is one that is complete with respect to all words contained therein (clue words and answers). Quality, cost effectiveness and coordination are primary concerns of both COMTIN units.

The cost of each puzzle depends on the size of the organization and is given in Table 2. A puzzle is solved by using the clues given to COMTIN A and B until the key word(s) can be completed. The key word(s) plus the clue words should be placed on Form K and submitted with the other completed portions of the original puzzle to the coordinator *prior to the end of the session in which it was acquired. Payment or credit for each completed puzzle is not received by the sub-unit heads until the beginning of the next period of play.* Heads of both sub-units will always receive equal shares of the COMTIN assets acquired by solving puzzles.

COMTIN assets (maintained by the coordinator) will be increased through puzzle completions according to Table 2. Essentially, COMTIN will receive for each solved puzzle 200% of the cost of the blank puzzle, and this money will be divided equally and added to the asset accounts of COMTIN A and COMTIN B.

COMTIN puzzles vary in difficulty, but there are on average one chance in five of buying a puzzle that has no solution. This does not necessarily mean that in any given performance period, you will be able to solve exactly four out of five puzzles. It might be that in some periods you will not be able to solve any of the puzzles; but in the long run about 80% will be solvable. The coordinator will sell blank puzzles in a predetermined, random order over which he or she has no control. The head of COMTIN A or B may withdraw part or all of that subunit's assets from the asset account maintained by the coordinator whenever he or she wishes by filling out Form I and presenting it to the coordinator. Also, Form I may be used to deposit Org$ in COMTIN's asset pools. These assets as well as

TABLE 2. Summary of COMTIN Assets, Income, Costs, and Payoffs[a] (in Org$)

Size	Starting Assets		Income in First Session[b]		Cost per Puzzle[c]	Increase in Assets for Solved Puzzle	
	A	B	A	B		A	B
One	50	50	5	5	40	40	40
Two	80	80	8	8	60	60	60

[a]*Probability of buying an unsolvable puzzle = 20%.*
[b]*Thereafter COMTIN A and B receive 10% (or as adjusted depending on the values of the performance indicators—see pp. 34-35) of their respective asset pools distributed to the unit head at the beginning of each session.*
[c]*For COMTIN A and COMTIN B combined.*

the income they generate (10% each period, or as adjusted depending on the values of the performance indicators; see pp. 38-40) may be used to buy puzzles or for other purposes.

The subunits of COMTIN, like ROUTIN, will have insufficient income and assets at the beginning to buy five puzzles. They will need to raise money from other parts of the organization if they wish to buy the maximum number of available puzzles.

Any task assignments made by the heads of COMTIN A or B must be formalized by submitting a Unit Task Assignment Schedule (Form G), or revision thereof, with appropriate fees, through EMREL to the coordinator. Base wage tickets, as well as dismissal forms, should also be handled through EMREL.

Effects on Organizational Performance Indicators

Puzzle purchases and solutions affect all four indicators of organizational performance (see Table 3, p. 41). The resource base is reduced for each puzzle acquired, but total output, internal cohesion, and member commitment are increased for each puzzle solved. Thus, the task activities of the subunits of COMTIN represent a short-term drain on the organization's resource base but add to other aspects of long-term organizational effectiveness.

Suggested Roles in COMTIN Sub-units

1. *Chief Accountant:* Someone responsible for managing COMTIN funds.

2. *Work Team Leader:* Someone responsible for the efforts directed at puzzle solution.

3. *Quality Analyst:* Someone responsible for tracking and evaluating the effectiveness of unit task operations.

4. *Integrator:* Someone responsible for coordinating the efforts of COMTIN A and B.

5. *Worker:* Someone responsible for doing the work on puzzles.

6. Other roles as deemed appropriate. *Be creative.*

CRUNODE (pronounced "crū'-nōde")

Overall Objective

To gather information useful to the organization and to make such information available to various organizational units.

What CRUNODE Does

CRUNODE, located in the Blue Division, is the organizational unit for information gathering, processing, and disseminating. At the beginning of each performance period, the coordinator will make available to the head of CRUNODE (a) the values of the performance indicators for the previous period; (b) the number of absences, new task assignments, quits, dismissals, vacations, job losses due to base wage failure, and members who are permanently and temporarily idle at the end of the previous period; (c) the input-output performance for the task units; and (d) the amounts of investments in Organizational Improvement or Human Resource Development. This information may be used by the head of CRUNODE in any way he or she sees fit, except that CRUNODE must maintain a concise record of these statistics for use at the end of play. This information provides the basis for assessing quality and effectiveness of the organization.

CRUNODE is also charged with the responsibility for disseminating information throughout the organization, and its members may use their discretion in deciding how to accomplish this function. For example, CRUNODE may wish to pass along its costs to consumers of its information or it may simply decide to absorb its costs of operation.

In addition, CRUNODE is responsible for completing Form V each session and submitting it to the coordinator *before* the end of each session. If this is accomplished, the internal cohesion performance indicator will be increased by two units for that session; if CRUNODE fails to perform this responsibility on time, the same indicator will decline by three units for that session.

As with other basic operating units, the head of CRUNODE will receive the unit's income at the beginning of each new performance period.

Any task assignments made by the head of CRUNODE must be formalized by submitting a Unit Task Assignment Schedule (Form G), or revision thereof, with appropriate fees, through EMREL to the coordinator. Base wage tickets as well as dismissal forms should also be handled through EMREL.

Suggested Roles in CRUNODE

1. *Information Monitor:* Someone responsible for monitoring critical organizational activities and for gathering information about them in a timely and accurate manner.

2. *Information Analyst:* Someone responsible for converting the information gathered into a form usable to other members and units and for maintaining a record of organizational events and statistics.

3. *Information Communicator:* Someone responsible for communicating or ensuring that CRUNODE information is communicated to the appropriate members or units in the organization.

4. Other roles as deemed appropriate. *Be creative.*

Income Budgeted for Each Performance Session

These following figures will be adjusted depending upon the values of the performance indicators each session (see pp. 38-41).

Size One:	$40
Size Two:	$60

EMREL *(pronounced "ĕm'-rĕl")*

Overall Objective

To oversee the task selection, placement, and dismissal of members. To manage the overall compensation plan and diversity initiatives of the organization. To manage all paperwork and reports associated with these processes. Also, to attempt to handle members' complaints that are unresolved at the unit level.

What EMREL Does

EMREL, located in the Blue Division, must organize the effort to staff the organization with the appropriate mix of human resources, drawing upon the diversity of all organization members. Although all participants are initially regarded as organizational members, as in any organization members must be appropriately matched to the tasks that must be performed. In fact, those who experience idleness for long periods of time run the risk of being unable to contribute in a meaningful way to the accomplishment of organizational goals.

All task assignments and dismissals of members must be coordinated through and authenticated by EMREL officials. All forms for these purposes, originating in the operating units, must be signed and delivered to the coordinator by an authorized official of EMREL before the end of the period in which they are initiated. (The EMREL signature does not imply consent or authorization; it merely signifies knowledge of the event.)

Specifically, before the end of each session, EMREL must:

1. Consolidate the list of those persons who can provide for their base subsistence wage and submit a Base Wage Report (Form S) and appropriate base wage tickets to the coordinator. (*Note:* Form S should include in alphabetical order names of all organization members and an indication of those having base wage each session.)

2. Consolidate the task assignments and dismissals, as evidenced by signed, authenticated, and fee-paid Forms G and O and submit these forms and fees, along with a Task Assignment Status Report (Form T), to the coordinator. (*Note:* Form T should include in alphabetical order names of all organization members and an indication of those having a task assignment each session. Also, the unit symbol should be circled for the person who is unit head.)

EMREL must attempt to determine the staffing needs of the operating units and to find members who can meet those needs. Members may attempt to influence directly the task assignment process and those who control it or they may rely on EMREL for these services; but, in any event, all changes in their task assignment status must be processed by EMREL.

EMREL may find it advantageous to arrange interviews for members with prospective task unit personnel. If members must travel to do this, EMREL may attempt to assist them in obtaining communication tickets for this purpose. If a member is to be assigned to a new task unit, EMREL must convey a $5 fee per new assignee from the task unit to which the member is assigned to the coordinator. This applies to reassignments and assignments after dismissals, quits, and job losses, as well as to initial task assignments. For all task assignments, EMREL must co-sign Form G with the appropriate unit heads. Likewise, if a unit dismisses a task performer, such an action must be acknowledged by an EMREL official who will convey a $5 dismissal expense from the dismissing unit to the coordinator. EMREL must co-sign Form O with unit heads. EMREL officials are responsible for delivering these forms, with appropriate expenses and a Task Assignment Status Report (Form T), to the coordinator before the end of the session in which they take place. Form T summarizes both initial task assignments and changes in task assignments, and it must include an alphabetized list of all organization members.

EMREL must submit a Base Wage Report (Form S) to the coordinator before the end of each session, accompanied by base wage tickets for each member. Form S must include an alphabetized list of all organization members. It will be initialed by the coordinator and returned to EMREL at the beginning of the next session.

EMREL may also be called upon to play a role in settling labor-management disputes.

Finally, EMREL may attempt to initiate other programs designed to enhance the employee selection and placement process within the organization, capitalizing on the diversity of the members.

EMREL may defray the expenses associated with its activities either through its internal budget or through assessments to operating units, or both.

Suggested Roles in EMREL

1. *Interviewer:* Someone responsible for interviewing and placing members into appropriate tasks within the basic operating units of the organization.

2. *Opportunity Analyst:* Someone responsible for determining and communicating the task performance needs of the basic operating units of the organization.

3. *Pay Administrator:* Someone responsible for administering the compensation plan, the forms and fees associated with member task assignments and dismissals, and the disposition of temporarily idle members (i.e., assuming that base wage tickets are turned in for them so they do not become permanently idle).

4. *Human Resource Analyst:* Someone responsible for implementing any programs designed to deal with human resource development, such as diversity, affirmative action, and training.

5. Other roles as deemed appropriate. *Be creative.*

Income Budgeted for Each Performance Session

The following figures will be adjusted depending upon the values of the performance indicators each session (see pp. 38-41).

Size One: $40
Size Two: $60

DECODE (pronounced "dē'-cōde")

Overall Objective

To serve as a change agent group.

What DECODE Does

DECODE, located in the Green Division, serves as an internal change agent group and in an advisory capacity to management. Its members may elect to initiate Total Quality Management efforts and undertake studies of organizational problems and culture for the purpose of making recommendations, developing plans, and assisting in the implementation of strategies and programs designed to enhance the effectiveness of the organization and the outcomes of its members. Form J can be used by DECODE to report on any organizational issues and recommended solutions. Members of DECODE may decide how they want to use this information in the organization, but a copy of the completed Form J must be given to the coordinator before the end of each session. If the form is submitted before the end of the session, Total Output and Member Cohesion performance indicators will be increased by two units for that session; otherwise, these indicators will be decreased by three units each, for that session.

Any task assignments made by the head of DECODE must be formalized by submitting a Unit Task Assignment Schedule (Form G), or revision thereof, with appropriate fees, through EMREL to the coordinator. Base wage tickets, as well as dismissal forms, should also be handled through EMREL.

Suggested Roles in DECODE

1. *Internal Consultants:* Persons responsible for conducting studies of current organizational problems and culture.
2. *Change Agent:* Someone responsible for implementing new programs.
3. *Program Evaluator:* Someone responsible for evaluating the effects of new programs and for providing feedback to management.

4. *Total Quality Manager:* Someone responsible for a Total Quality program for the organization

5. Other roles as deemed appropriate. *Be creative.*

Income Budgeted for Each Performance Session

The following figures will be adjusted depending upon the values of the performance indicators each session (see pp. 38-41).

Size One:	$40
Size Two:	$60

COPE (pronounced "cōpe")

Overall Objective

To manage the internal finances of the organization.

What COPE Does

Located in the Green Division, COPE is responsible for the development and management of the internal finances of the organization, and it serves in an advisory capacity to management. Its members are responsible for accounting and financial analysis functions and may engage in problem-solving activities within this general domain. Form U should be used by COPE to keep track of the organization's financial status on a session-by-session basis. This information may be obtained and used in whatever ways are deemed appropriate by COPE members. But a copy of Form U must be given to the coordinator before the end of each session. If this is done, the Resource Base performance indicator will be increased by two units for that session; if the form is not turned in before the close of a session, the Resource Base indicator will decline by three units for that session.

Any task assignments made by the head of COPE must be formalized by submitting a Unit Task Assignment Schedule (Form G), or revision thereof, with appropriate fees, through EMREL to the coordinator. Base wage tickets, as well as dismissal forms, should also be handled through EMREL.

Suggested Roles in COPE

1. *Accountant:* Someone responsible for keeping track of the financial status of the organization.

2. *Financial Analyst:* Someone responsible for analyzing financial transactions and conducting cost-benefit studies.

3. *Production Analyst:* Someone responsible for analyzing the production efficiency of the task units.

4. Other roles as deemed appropriate. *Be creative.*

Income Budgeted for Each Performance Session

The following figures will be adjusted depending upon the values of the performance indicators each session (see pp. 38-41).

Size One: $40
Size Two: $60

HOPE (pronounced "hōpe")

Overall Objective

To engage major issues confronting the organization and to develop programs and mobilize supporters for this purpose.

What HOPE Does

When *The Game* begins, HOPE, located in the Red Division, is a unit without a well-defined program, goal, or philosophy. It is up to its members to identify important issues within the organization and to develop agenda and programs for resolving these issues. However, two specific responsibilities that are assigned to HOPE are to ensure that people find a job in the organization and to work for the good of the total membership of the organization.

Any task assignments made by the head of HOPE must be formalized by submitting a Unit Task Assignment Schedule (Form G), or revision thereof, with appropriate fees, through EMREL to the coordinator. Base wage tickets, as well as dismissal forms, should also be handled through EMREL.

Suggested Roles in HOPE

1. *Program Director:* Someone responsible for developing the unit's philosophy and program.
2. *Membership Director:* Someone responsible for mobilizing support from members for the unit and its programs.
3. *Task Force Leader:* Someone responsible for achieving the unit's tasks.
4 . Other roles as deemed appropriate. *Be creative.*

Income Budgeted for Each Performance Session

The following figures will be adjusted depending upon the values of the performance indicators each session (see pp. 38-41).

Size One:	$40
Size Two:	$60

Unit Heads

Unit heads are initially assigned by the coordinator at the beginning of play. Since they are then task assigned, no hiring fee is needed for them, but their names must appear on Forms S and T. *Also, they must receive a base wage ticket for each session or they will lose their position as unit head, and the income to the unit will be lost until a new head is appointed by the organization members.*

Powers of Unit Heads

Unit heads may assign or dismiss organizational members from the performance of tasks within their domain on any terms they wish and for any reasons, so long as these actions are formally coordinated through EMREL. The unit's basic income is delivered to its head at the beginning of each period. The head also exercises control over the unit's assets.

The unit head has signature authority for the unit on matters of asset withdrawals and deposits (Form I), member task assignments (Form G), and dismissals (Form O). No individual will be considered assigned to or dismissed from the unit without the express consent of its head. An individual may quit a unit task by informing the relevant unit head and EMREL of his or her decision through the use of Form P. Finally, agreements on salary (beyond the mandatory base wage) and working conditions are internal matters between the head and the member.

Replacing Unit Heads

1. *Voluntary removal:* The head of a unit may resign at any time and suggest a successor to the other members and to EMREL.
2. *Involuntary removal:* The unit head is automatically removed when any of the following conditions are met:
    A. If absent for a session (i.e., more than five minutes late).
    B. If no base wage is secured for a session, either by ticket or by certificate.
    C. By unanimous consent (signatures) of all of the other unit heads.
    D. By unanimous consent (signatures) of all of the unit employees.
3. *Replacement procedures:* The unit head may be replaced by the following procedures (please note that until the unit head is replaced, the unit will receive *no* income):
    A. If the unit head voluntarily resigns or if he or she is removed by being absent, by not securing base wage, or by unanimous consent of the unit employees, the unit employees must decide on a replacement and forward a revised Form G through EMREL to the coordinator during the period in which replacement occurs. If there are no other employees in the unit, then the members of the division where the unit is located must select the new unit head.
    B. If the unit head is dismissed by the remaining alternative—that is, by the unanimous consent of all other unit heads—a replacement will be chosen by the other existing unit heads. The other unit heads must decide on a replacement and forward a revised Form G through EMREL to the coordinator during the period in which replacement occurs.

Stating Your Preferences

Before beginning to play *The Game,* tear out your Choice Sheet (Form A) from the front of this manual and indicate your preferences for the role of unit head. Put only your name on the Assignment Sheet (Form B). Both forms must be turned in to the coordinator before play. The coordinator will complete Form B and return it to you at the beginning of the first session of the simulation.

The selection process for unit heads is straightforward. Among those who list a first choice for a particular unit, one player will be assigned to head that group. If there are no first choices for a unit, second and third choices will prevail. Several members will be assigned to be controllers; all other members will be assigned to the four divisions and must seek a task assignment in one of the basic operating units. In seeking assignment:

1. You do not have to join the unit you originally indicated as your preferred unit on Form A, but you may join any unit with which you can negotiate a task assignment.

2. You can work for *only one unit*, at least insofar as Form G (Unit Task Assignment Schedule) is concerned. Formal assignment, signified by the Form G listing, will entitle you to receive as a minimum a base wage from your unit head. You may, however, have a temporary or informal assignment with another unit or perform other duties under informal arrangements; but you may not be listed on more than one Unit Task Assignment Schedule at a time.

Absenteeism

When a member of the organization is absent because of an employee "walkout" or any other reason, no base wages need to be presented to the coordinator. If the person absent is a unit head, that position is automatically lost, the person goes to the Red Division to become temporarily idle at the beginning of the next session, and a new unit head is appointed according to the above instructions. Employees other than unit heads retain their assignments unless they are dismissed by the unit head and are not considered temporarily idle. However, the organization will not receive the base wage tickets, communication tickets, or Org$ due the absentee for the session involved. *A member is considered absent five minutes after the performance session begins.*

In addition to these personal consequences, all of the Performance Indicators will be adversely affected by absences. For every member absent from any period regardless of the reason, Resource Base, Total Output, and Member Commitment will be reduced by two units and Internal Cohesion will *be* reduced by three units.

For any period in which there are five or more absentees (but fewer than ten), income for the basic units will be reduced by 10%. If 10 or more are absent income for the basic units will be reduced another 10%, and so forth. Also, one of the base wage controllers' tickets (p. 31) will be eliminated for each increment of 5 absences.

Task Assignments

Each player is considered to be a member of the organization. However, one may be a member of an organization with little if anything constructive to do. Thus, the term *task assignment* will be used here in the restrictive sense to identify those members who hold meaningful jobs in one of the basic operating units. Evidence of this status is the appearance of your name on a Unit Task Assignment Schedule (Form G), and all task assignments must be formally processed through EMREL (Form T) in order to be valid. Until members are formally task assigned, they are considered "temporarily idle." When a person is assigned a task, he or she is automatically transferred to the division containing the task unit to which he or she is assigned, whether this is the first task or a reassignment.

Organizational members may hold only one formal task assignment at any given time during the play of *The Organization Game.* That is, they may appear on only one Unit Task Assignment Schedule at a time. They may, however, perform a number of other part-time or informal tasks in the same unit or in other units for which they may or may not be compensated. But these statuses are not reported on a Unit Task Assignment Schedule.

Organizational members may work on their own or in conjunction with EMREL in an effort to obtain an assignment in one of the major operating units of the organization. Regardless of how this status is obtained, a $5 fee along with a completed or revised Form G must be forwarded through appropriate channels to the coordinator. This $5 assignment fee also covers the transfer cost to the new division for the first task assignment, a reassignment, or an assignment after dismissal, quitting, or loss of task.

Finally, the task unit must provide as a minimum a base wage ticket or certificate for all individuals listed on its Unit Task Assignment Schedule during each period of play. Above this minimum wage, it is up to each employee and the task unit to negotiate a fair compensation package, using Org$ or other means of compensation. If no base wage ticket is submitted for a person with a task, the person loses the task, becomes temporarily idle, and is assigned to the Red Division.

New task assignment occurs when a member is initially assigned a task, is reassigned to a new task, or is assigned a task after being dismissed or quitting. A person may also be reassigned to a task if he or she lost a previous task because no base wage had been submitted for a session. New task assignment has an impact on the performance indicators (see Table 3, p. 42). Whereas each new assignment increases the Resource Base by one unit, it causes a decline by one unit in both Total Output and Internal Cohesion as these newcomers are being assimilated into the task unit. Thus, the assignment of members to unit tasks is absolutely essential if the organization is adequately to perform its operations, but the process of selection and placement incurs certain short-term expenses that may be offset by stable performance thereafter.

Dismissals and Quits

A member may be dismissed from his or her unit task for unsatisfactory performance as determined by the unit head. Also, a member may decide to quit the unit task. In either event, the coordinator must be notified in a particular manner. In the case of a dismissal, the unit head must file Form O, bearing his or her signature and the acknowledging signature of an EMREL official, along with a $5 dismissal expense, with the coordinator. Members quitting their unit task must file Form P with the coordinator (EMREL co-signature not required). In addition, base wage failure for a member who has a task assignment or who is a unit head results in that member being automatically dismissed. Unit heads who are absent are also automatically dismissed.

A member who quits or is dismissed from a unit task is considered temporarily idle and must immediately move to the Red Division. Loss of task assignment does not prohibit the member from negotiating a base wage for ordinary organizational membership to avoid being placed in the permanently idle category. In fact, the member is encouraged to do so to avoid this status in the next session of play.

Each dismissal or quit lowers all of the performance indicators for the session in which it occurs (see Table 3, p. 42). In addition, each of these events also means the individual is temporarily idle (see p. 32-33), and this too has an impact on the performance indicators.

Base Wages

In order to remain a viable member of the organization, each player must, for every session in which present, provide for his or her own subsistence. A member must do this either by (a) submitting a base wage ticket to EMREL, who will turn in a Base Wage Report (Form S) along with the required base wage tickets before the end of each period of play; or (b) purchasing a permanent base wage certificate from the coordinator, which covers his or her base wage for the present session as well as for all future sessions of *The Organization Game*, and informing EMREL of this purchase.

Permanent Base Wage Certificate

Any organizational member may purchase a permanent base wage certificate from the coordinator at any time during a session at a cost of $25 (Form E). He or she may transfer the certificate to another player (Form F), but a transfer expense of $3 must be paid to the coordinator. Finally, the permanent base wage certificate can be used to provide for only one player per session.

Base Wage Controller

As in the case of Communication Ticket Controllers, a certain number of players will be designated as Base Wage Controllers during the initial assignment of roles in *The Organization Game*. The number of controllers depends on the size of the organization, which the coordinator announces at the beginning of play. These controllers will each receive five base wage tickets in each session, which they can use as they choose. Unused base wage tickets may be carried over from session to session, and the duties of the base wage controller, as well as the session's supply of five tickets, may be transferred to another person, but a transfer charge of $3 must be given to the coordinator along with a completed Form F. If a base wage controller is absent, his or her supply of base wage tickets is lost to the organization for that session. Base Wage Controllers are considered to have a formal task assignment, but they may not employ others. Since controllers are considered task assigned, no hiring fee is needed for them, but their names must appear on Forms S and T. Also, they must receive a base wage ticket for each session or lose their position as controller and be sent to the Red Division. Finally, the controller is permanently assigned to his or her original division.

Failure to Provide Base Wage

Failure to provide base wages for members has various consequences depending on how long this condition lasts.

   If a member fails to receive a base wage for a session in which he or she had no formal task assignment, that member will be considered temporarily idle for that session. If a person had a task assignment or was a controller or a unit head, failure to secure base wage means that that assignment will be nullified and the player will automatically be assigned to the Red Division and considered temporarily idle for that session. A new head or controller must then be chosen (see p. 27), and until someone is chose the unit will receive no income.

   The *temporarily idle* label and the assignment to the Red Division remain in effect until the member provides a base wage ticket or purchases a permanent base wage certificate and secures a new task assignment.

Although members may not engage in official transactions when temporarily idle, they may talk with others, communicate across inter-division boundaries, and even transfer from one division to another if they have the means. The member's first priority should be to secure a base wage, with or without a formal task assignment, to avoid becoming permanently idle. He or she does not automatically assume the previous assignment when base wages are regained, however. Form G must be completed and accompanied by a $5 fee in order for a member to be reassigned to a task.

The impact of base wage failure on the organizational performance indicators depends on the task assignment of the member at the beginning of the period in which failure occurs. If the member had a formal task assignment, base wage failure is more severe because it results in temporary idleness that affects the indicators (see Table 3, p. 42) and assignment to the Red Division. If the member was not engaged in a formal task assignment at the time of base wage failure, temporary idleness occurs or is prolonged (see Table 3, p. 42, for impact on performance indicators).

Repeated Base Wage Failure

If base wage failure occurs for a member in two consecutive sessions, the member is considered *permanently idle,* and his or her services will be permanently withdrawn from the organization. In essence, if a member's services are not regarded by other members as sufficiently valuable to justify a mere base wage, that player runs the risk of being placed in a permanently idle job classification. A base wage may be awarded to a member with no formal task assignment in the interest of keeping the organization together.

Permanently Idle and

Temporarily Idle

Organizational members who do not secure a base wage or who do not find a formal task assignment, or both, run the risk of being placed in either the *permanently idle* or *temporarily idle* job categories.

Any member failing to provide a base subsistence wage for any session is automatically placed in the temporarily idle category. Also, any members whose names do not appear on a Unit Task Assignment Schedule (Form G) and/or on EMREL's master Task Assignment Status Report (Form T) are considered to be temporarily idle. In other words, one must have both a task assignment and a base wage to avoid being temporarily idle. Members assigned to a task who do not receive a base wage for a session suffer temporary idleness and assignment to the Red Division. Members not having a task are considered temporarily idle for the session in which failure to provide base wage occurs.

It is conceivable that a member may be stuck in a temporarily idle category for several sessions of play. However, if a member fails to provide for his or her base subsistence wage for two consecutive sessions, that member may be placed in a permanently idle job category. Each person who becomes permanently idle may be removed from play and will be asked to assist the coordinator during the remainder of the simulation.

It is to the joint advantage of the individual and the organization to avoid events that lead to members becoming permanently idle. The effects on the performance indicators are shown in Table 3 (p. 42).

Options

The coordinator will announce whether any of the following options are in effect.

E-Mail Option

If computer facilities permit, the coordinator may announce that you can pay a fee per session ($25) to use a computer network to communicate via e-mail between divisions.

Vacation Option

A vacation entitles a member to be away from the organization for a whole session of play without losing his or her organizational privileges or positions during the absence. A vacation form (Form Q) must be filed by the member with the coordinator during the session immediately prior to the one in which a vacation is sought. This form must be signed by the unit head (if the vacationer is not a unit head) and must be acknowledged by the signature of an EMREL official. It must be accompanied by a charge of $10 and a base wage ticket to cover the session away from the organization. If the vacationer is a unit head or controller, he or she must designate an acting unit head or controller during the vacation. For each member taking a vacation there is a negative effect on three of the performance indicators (see Table 3, p. 42).

Communication Ticket Purchase Option

Any member of the organization may purchase a communication ticket good for one visit to all other divisions. A payment of $4 to the coordinator is all that is required to obtain the ticket.

Job Protection Ticket Option

A job protection ticket (Form W) may be purchased from the coordinator for a charge of $15 by any member of the organization. This ticket protects the holder from arbitrary dismissal from his or her job by the unit head. When a person holds a job protection ticket, dismissal can only occur when all unit heads agree that dismissal is justified and sign the Dismissal Form (Form O) to signify their agreement. When the job protection ticket holder is a unit head, dismissal agreement must come from all other unit heads and carries a severance cost of $10 to the dismissed unit head.

Highest Savings Award Option

At the end of every third session, each person who is not a unit head uses the Savings Award Form (Form X) to report to the coordinator the total number of Org$ in his or her envelope. The member having the largest savings will receive an award equal to 10% of his or her total savings, or a free base wage ticket. The winner will be notified at the beginning of the next session and given a chance to exercise his or her option.

Compensation Plan Option

By the end of the third session, DECODE must develop a performance appraisal and compensation system for all members of the organization. This system would include a plan for personnel evaluation and a description of how people will be paid over and above their base wages (that is, in Org$). The plan must be approved and initialed by all unit heads and a copy turned in to the coordinator. Otherwise, beginning with the fourth session, all performance indicators will automatically decline by 15% each session.

Other Options

Other options may be announced by the coordinator during the play of *The Organization Game.*

Individual Goals

The organization will be more interesting and realistic if, in addition to various group goals and organizational goals, persons are pursuing one or more individual goals at the same time.

A short list of suggested individual goals is given below. You should choose one or more of these (or others if you prefer) to pursue from the beginning, and you may change your personal goals once the simulation begins. In addition, you do not have to communicate these goals to anyone else, but to track your objectives during the game, you should make note of your choice at the beginning of play and at any time you change your goals.

The following list may stimulate you to identify a personal goal for the play of *The Organization Game:*

1. *Power.* I will try to influence what happens in the organization as much as possible.

2. *Center of attention.* I will try to be a central figure in the organization, important to as many people as possible.

3. *Personal benefits.* I will try to enjoy the highest salary and other benefits possible. I will treat myself to personal pleasures at my convenience.

4. *Security.* I will try to lead an existence where I will have the most job security possible and will not be threatened by the possibility of dismissal.

5. *Growth.* I will seek out those opportunities for personal growth and development in the organization.

6. *Achievement.* I will try to be the most proficient producer in the organization.

7. *Affiliation.* I will try to be liked by everyone in the organization and to work effectively with everyone.

8. *Other.* Specify your own goal, but be sure it is for you as an individual and not for the unit or division in which you have membership or for the total organization.

Some information may be available from the Assessment Form (Form N), which will help you to evaluate your success in achieving your individual goals.

Performance Indicators

At the end of each session, the coordinator calculates numerical values for four organizational performance indicators as one means of measuring the general effectiveness of the organization as a whole. Each indicator pertains to a different feature of organizational life, and, in general, a high numerical score indicates greater organizational effectiveness.

In a very real sense, enhancement of the indicators means that as a group you have been able to organize and manage the multitude of internal and external factors impinging upon your organization. You will find also that, as in real life, actions leading to the enhancement of one or more of these indicators may have a negative impact on others (e.g., in order to produce you must draw from your resource base; in order to enhance member commitment to the organization, you may have to divert energy away from the primary tasks of your organization; and so forth).

The four performance indicators are as follows:

1. *Resource Base.* The fundamental question answered by this indicator: Is your organization replenishing the resources that it consumes? Effectiveness on this dimension is due, in part, to your ability to perform the organization's tasks effectively so as to minimize depletion of resources through unnecessary waste. Another major part can be attributed to the decisions you make regarding the allocation of funds within the organization given many competing alternatives. A lower resource base score means that decisions being made in your organization are causing a drain on its resource base.

2. *Total Output.* The fundamental question answered by this indicator: Is your organization maintaining a high rate of output in the production of goods or the delivery of services? Many factors will contribute to output effectiveness, including the extent to which your organization reinvests in its material and human resources. Whereas total output is increased by the completion of ROUTIN and COMTIN tasks, it will be adversely affected by an uncooperative work force. A higher total output score means greater output effectiveness.

3. *Internal Cohesion.* This is an indicator of *the extent to* which organizational members function as an integrated whole. The fundamental question answered by this indicator: What is the state of collaboration between individuals and groups in your organization? Efforts at human resource development may be expected to enhance this indicator, whereas unsatisfactory matches between people and jobs in the organization will decrease internal cohesion. A higher internal cohesion score means that fewer destructive conflicts are present in the organization.

4. *Member Commitment.* This indicator represents the degree of commitment members have to the organization. It answers the question: Are there many people in the organization who are dissatisfied with its functioning, structure, or values? Member commitment is influenced by the degree of investment in human resources development and is lowered by indices having to do with psychological or physical withdrawal of members from active participation in the organization. The higher the score on member commitment, the greater the organizational commitment of the members.

Reinvestment in Organization

The performance indicators may be raised by investing Org$ in either the Organizational Improvement (OI) Program or the Human Resource Development (HRD) Program, as well as by the performance and operations of the organization and its parts. Org$ may be invested in these programs by submitting a completed Form R1 for the OI Program or Form R2 for the HRD Program to the coordinator with the appropriate amount of Org$. Once money is invested in these programs, it cannot later be withdrawn from the resource pool. These investments are sunk costs. The two programs are as follows:

1. *Organizational Improvement* (OI). This program constitutes a reinvestment in the organization, ostensibly to improve production processes and the utilization of material resources. It directly affects both resource base and total output in a positive manner. An OI investment should be based upon an actual plan to improve production by ROUTIN and COMTIN A and B. Indeed, its impact on the resource base and total output is affected by the number of anagrams and puzzles solved in the following session. If the combined total of anagrams and puzzles solved is greater than or equal to eight, the resource base will increase by .2 of a unit for each dollar invested in OI, and total output will increase by .1 of a unit for each dollar invested in OI. If the combined total of anagrams and puzzles is less than eight, the resource base is increased by .1 of a unit and total output by .05 of a unit for each dollar invested in OI. These effects on the resource base and total output take effect at the end of the session following the session in which the OI investment is made.

2. *Human Resource Development* (HRD). This program represents an investment in the organization's human resources. It may be conveniently thought of as being designed to improve the technical, team, and/or interpersonal skills of the organization's members. Given these objectives, investments in HRD will increase the total output, internal cohesion, and member commitment indicators of organizational effectiveness.

Investments in HRD are required to be accompanied by a written plan for actual HRD activities that will be implemented. For every $100 (or fraction thereof) invested in HRD, the organization must provide some human resources activity. Some possible actions include (a) instituting a periodic survey of employees' attitudes, (b) developing a team building plan for the organization, (c) creating a bonus plan for employees to receive bonus Org$ or communication tickets, (d) devising a program for awarding certificates of excellence to employees, and (e) developing a plan for capitalizing on diversity in the organization. The impact of the HRD investments on the performance indicators is as follows: total output increased by .1 of a unit for each dollar invested in HRD; internal cohesion and member commitment each increased by .2 of a unit for each dollar invested in HRD. These effects will take place at the end of the session following the session in which the HRD investment is made, assuming Form R3 is completed and turned in to report the human resources activity prescribed (otherwise the investment has no effect).

Investments in these programs may be made by any member, unit, group, or coalition in the organization, using Forms R1 and R2, except that investments in HRD must be approved by five of the unit heads. The effects of these investments on the four organizational performance indicators of Resource Base, Total Output, Internal Cohesion, and Member Commitment are summarized below. *Their effects are realized at the end of the session of play following the one in which the investment is made.*

Any group or individual may decide to aid the organization by advising its members on policies regarding organizational structure and operations, investment policies, employee matters, and any other matters that may directly or indirectly affect the performance indicators and contribute to the effectiveness of the organization.

Changes in the Performance Indicators

At the beginning of *The Game*, all four indicators of performance are given an initial value of 100. Thereafter, all indicators decline automatically at the rate of 10% per session unless otherwise affected by the activities of the organization's members. An organization must expend "energy" to maintain itself, even though its members are doing nothing.

Investments in the OI and HRD Programs cause an increase in the performance indicators, but these programs have administrative costs and are not 100% effective. Thus, an Org$ invested in them does not bring an equivalent rise in the performance indicators.

More specifically, indicators can be changed in the following ways:

1. Resource Base
   A. Raised by 20% or 10% (depending on production level) of the value of all new Org$ invested in the OI Program (takes effect one session after investment is made).
   B. Lowered by one unit for each anagram purchased by ROUTIN and two units for each puzzle purchased by COMTIN.
   C. Raised by one unit for each member assigned to a new task.
   D. Lowered by two units for each member absent.
   E. Lowered by three units for each member who is dismissed or who quits a unit.
   F. Lowered by one unit for each member who takes a vacation.
   G. Lowered by one unit for each member who is temporarily idle.
   H. Raised by two units for each session report turned in by COPE; lowered by three units if the report is not turned in.

2. Total Output
   A. Raised by 10% or 5% (depending on production level) of any new Org$ invested in the OI Program (takes effect one session after the investment is made).
   B. Raised by 10% of any new Org$ invested in the HRD Program, depending on implementation of a real HRD activity (takes effect one session after investment is made).
   C. Raised by three units for each word completed by ROUTIN and by four units for each puzzle solved by COMTIN.
   D. Lowered by one unit for each member assigned to a new task.
   E. Lowered by two units for each member absent.
   F. Lowered by three units for each member who is dismissed or who quits a unit.
   G. Lowered by one unit for each member who takes a vacation.
   H. Lowered by one unit for each member who is temporarily idle.
   I. Raised by two units for each session report turned in by DECODE; lowered by three units if the report is not turned in.

3. Internal Cohesion
   A. Raised by 20% of any new Org$ invested in the HRD Program, depending on implementation of a real HRD activity (takes effect one session after the investment is made).
   B. Raised by two units for each puzzle solved by COMTIN.
   C. Lowered by one unit for each member assigned to a new task.
   D. Lowered by three units for each member absent.

    E. Lowered by three units for each member who is dismissed or who quits.

    F. Lowered by one unit for each member who takes a vacation.

    G. Lowered by three units for each member who becomes permanently idle.

    H. Lowered by one unit for each member who is temporarily idle.

    I. Raised by two units for each session report turned in by CRUNODE; lowered by three units if the report is not turned in.

4. Member Commitment

    A. Raised by 20% of any new Org$ invested in the HRD Program, depending on implementation of a real HRD activity (takes effect one session after investment is made).

    B. Raised by two units for each word completed by ROUTIN and by two units for each puzzle solved by COMTIN.

    C. Lowered by two units for each member absent.

    D. Lowered by three units for each member who is dismissed or who quits a unit.

    E. Lowered by five units for each member who becomes permanently idle.

    F. Lowered by one unit for each member who is temporarily idle.

    G. Raised by two units for each session report turned in by DECODE; lowered by three units if it is not turned in.

Table 3 on page 41 summarizes these effects on performance indicators.

Consequences of Different Values of Performance Indicators

The amount of income distributed to the heads of the basic units at the beginning of each period is affected by the values of the performance indicators as follows:

1. Every unit will receive 20% more than its basic income for any period in which *all* of the performance indicators are above 125 at the beginning of the period.

2. Every unit will receive 10% less than its basic income for any period in which any indicator is below 90; 20% less for any period in which any indicator is below 80; 30% less for any period in which any indicator is below 70; and so forth down to 90% less for any period in which any indicator is below 10. This applies to

ROUTIN and COMTIN as well, although their assets in the common resource pool, administered by the coordinator, are not affected. *The organization has failed if any performance indicator falls below zero.*

TABLE 3. Effects of Investments and Other Events on Performance Indicators (stated as % of Org$ invested or units per event)

Organizational Investments and Other Events	Organizational Performance Indicators			
	RB	TO	IC	MC
Investments	% of investment			
OI Program	+20 (10)[a]	+10 (5)[a]	0	0
HRD Program	0	+10[b]	+20[b]	+20[b]
Events	Units per event			
Anagrams purchased	-1	0	0	0
Puzzles purchased	-2	0	0	0
Anagrams completed	0	+3	0	+2
Puzzles solved	0	+4	+2	+2
New task assignee	+1	-1	-1	0
Absence	-2	-2	-3	-2
Dismissal/Quit	-3	-3	-3	-3
Vacation	-1	-1	-1	0
Permanently idle	0	0	-3	-5
Temporarily idle	-1	-1	-1	-1
COPE report turned in (not turned in)	+2 (-3)	0	0	0
DECODE report turned in (not turned in)	0	+2 (-3)	0	+2 (-3)
CRUNODE report turned in (not turned in)	0	0	+2 (-3)	0

Note: RB = resource base; TO = total output; IC = internal cohesion; MC = member commitment; OI = organizational improvement; HRD = human resource development.

[a]Percentage effect delayed one session. Percentage (20% or 10% for RB; 10% or 5% for TO) depends on number of anagrams and puzzles solved the session after the investment is made.

[b]Percentage effect delayed one session and depends on implementation of a real HRD activity.

Management Function

There is no formal requirement that the organization establish a general management function. However, if the members wish to set up such a function, they may do so at any time. If a management function is formed, organizational members may organize and manage it in any way they see fit, so long as no basic rules are violated.

Strikes

For better or worse, members of the organization sometimes reach an impasse in their work-related dealings with others. Such impasses may result in work slowdowns, grievances, or actual work stoppages.

Initiating a Strike

Any individual or group may withhold work, demand a hearing of their concerns, and at the same time be protected from dismissal through the creation of a strike. A strike is created by completing two copies of Form L and filing one with EMREL and one with the coordinator, along with a $25 fee. Form L requires a statement of grievance(s) that informs the coordinator of the grounds for the strike. This statement of grievance(s) must be unambiguous. Work stoppage may or may not be involved in a strike, and this should be made clear on Form L. The coordinator will announce to all divisions that a strike has been initiated, and it is EMREL's responsibility to give copies of Form L to the unit(s) employing the strike members.

A strike must be renewed before the end of the period following the one in which it is initiated and before the end of each subsequent period. Otherwise, the strike will automatically expire at the end of the period. A strike may be renewed by paying the coordinator a renewal fee of $10.

The strikers must also designate a leader for communication purposes unless the strike is initiated by one person. The leader of the strike has no special powers that other members of the strike do not have; he or she merely serves as the contact person for the strike.

A strike has two major objectives: (a) to require that grievances be resolved by the organization and (b) to protect its members from arbitrary dismissal.

Resolution of Grievances

Once a strike has been initiated, a representative of the employing unit(s) must meet with the leader of the strike, before the end of the period following strike initiation, in an effort to resolve the grievance(s). This meeting can take place anywhere in the organization and can involve up to one-half of the participants (recall the one-division capacity rule).

The meeting must involve bargaining in good faith by both sides. All must honestly attempt to resolve the grievance(s).

As many meetings as needed may be held to satisfy the strike members, and EMREL may be called upon to help resolve the grievance(s). The coordinator will not become involved in any of these meetings. If, however, the parties involved cannot reach a resolution after a concerted and extended effort, they may call upon the coordinator to hear both sides and to render a final decision, which will be binding upon both parties. Once the coordinator has rendered a decision, neither party may again raise this issue. For the coordinator to become involved, the organization and the strike members must both pay to the bank a fee of $100, or a total of $200, for this service. They must prepare their cases for presentation during the next break between periods.

At the meeting held with the coordinator during the break, each party will have five minutes to present its case, with the strike members going first. Each party will have two minutes to offer a rebuttal. The coordinator will then ask any necessary questions and retire to make a decision, which will be announced at the beginning of the next period. *It is definitely advantageous to the organization that the parties reach a resolution without having to resort to arbitration by the coordinator.*

Any person who is a member of a strike cannot be dismissed by a unit while the strike is in effect. All members of a strike are indicated on Form L, and that form will be used to determine who is protected by the strike. In addition, the strike may place any other individual under its protection by indicating that individual's name on Form L, but to be effective, protection must be extended to a person prior to the time the coordinator receives word that the person has been dismissed.

Dues and Fines

Members of a strike may wish to institute a schedule of dues and fines to help defray the expenses of their actions. The coordinator will not act as the collector or enforcer of such dues or fines. If dues or fines are assessed against someone who refuses to pay, members of the organization must decide how to handle the situation. In short, the collection of fines and dues is the responsibility of the players and will not be assumed by the coordinator.

Terminating a Strike

A strike is automatically in effect for one full period after the one in which it was originally formed. If renewed (use a new Form L), it remains in effect for one more period and this process must be repeated before the close of each period if the strike is to remain in effect for the next period. If it is not renewed, it ceases to exist at the beginning of the next period. A strike may also be removed by filing Form M, which has been signed by at least two-thirds of the strike members, with the coordinator. Such voluntary removal may be initiated in cases where the strike members decide that there is no need to continue the strike for its full limit.

If the strike involves a work stoppage, the strikers are considered absent, and their absence has the same impact on performance indicators as other absences. The organization may attempt to offset the effect of the strike by engaging other members of the organization to perform the work of the strike members. There is no expectation that a strike will necessarily occur. It is only a possibility, and the organization may end up with none, one, or several depending on the decisions of its members.

Special Events (Optional)

Sometime during the play of *The Organization Game,* the coordinator may announce the occurrence of certain outside special events affecting the organization. You will not know in advance when or if the events will occur or what their nature is until they occur. They are mentioned here so that you realize that they are part of the game and that the coordinator may use them to highlight specific learning opportunities.

Summary

The rules of *The Organization Game* are complex, and considerable effort on your part will be needed to acquire a working knowledge of them. Indeed, if they could be understood fully by one person after a couple of readings, a complex organization such as the one you're about to create would not be needed! Because of this organization, all of these details need not be mastered by every player. The uncertainties you now experience will subside in direct proportion to the effectiveness of the organization you and your peers create.

The basic question many people have at this initial stage is simply, What is the object of *The Game?* For you as a participant, there are several objectives:

1. To achieve the personal goal(s) you have set for yourself.
2. To help the basic unit or division in which you have a job to achieve its goals.
3. To see to it that the organization as a whole is a "success."

If you conscientiously try to achieve these objectives, the larger objective of learning about organizations and management will be achieved. To help you keep track of these objectives and to provide you with information on how you are doing, the coordinator may ask you to fill out and hand in an Assessment Form (Form N) during the course of the simulation. These will be occasions for you to take stock of your position and to plan for the future. In addition, you may find it helpful to keep a journal of key events as play unfolds. Finally, the organization may itself decide to collect information from time to time that may help you assess the accomplishment of the three objectives mentioned above.

Good luck! Have fun and learn about organizations and their management.

Part Two

Players' Forms

List of Player's Forms

A	Choice Sheet	i
B	Assignment Sheet	i
C	Division Transfer Sheet	51
D	Permanent Communication Certificate	51
E	Permanent Base Wage Certificate	51
F	Transfer of Certificates or Controllerships	53
G	Unit Task Assignment Schedule	55
H	ROUTIN Task Unit: Input-Output Form	61
I	Withdrawal/Deposit of Assets Form	65
J	DECODE Organizational Diagnosis Report	67
K	COMTIN Task Unit: Input-Output Form	71
L	Declaring a Strike	77
M	Strike Termination Form	79
N	Assessment Form	81
O	Dismissal Form	85
P	Quit Form	85
Q	Vacation Form	89
R1	OI Investment Form	91
R2	HRD Investment Form	93
R3	HRD Investment Report Form	95
S	EMREL Base Wage Report Form	97
T	EMREL Task Assignment Status Report	101
U	COPE Report of Financial Operations	105
V	CRUNODE Information Report	109
W	Job Protection Ticket	113
X	Savings Award Form	115

DIVISION TRANSFER SHEET

Please record the fact that _____ is moving from the:

(name)

| (circle one) | Red | Yellow | Blue | Green | Division | Initials of approving unit heads: |

_____

to the:

| (circle one) | Red | Yellow | Blue | Green | Division |

_____
_____
_____
_____

Expense: $5 (paid to coordinator)

— —

Form D

Session #_____

PERMANENT COMMUNICATION CERTIFICATE

This is to certify that _____ has purchased a permanent communication certificate

(name)

and is henceforth free to engage in interdivision communications for the duration of the simulation.

_____

(coordinator or assistant)

Expense: $25 (paid to coordinator)

— —

Form E

Session #_____

PERMANENT BASE WAGE CERTIFICATE

This is to certify that _____ has purchased a permanent base wage certificate

(name)

and henceforth is free from having to present a base wage ticket at the end of each performance session for the duration of the simulation.

_____

(coordinator or assistant)

Expense: $25 (paid to coordinator)

TRANSFER OF CERTIFICATES OR CONTROLLERSHIPS

This is to certify the transfer of: (circle one)

Base wage controllership   Permanent base wage certificate

Communication ticket controllership   Permanent communication certificate

From: _____
                 (Old controller/owner)

To: _____
              (New controller/owner)

_____
(Old controller/owner)

_____
(New controller/owner)

(Note: To use transferred certificates, present this form with the original certificate to the coordinator.)

_____
(coordinator or assistant)

Transfer expense: $3 (paid to coordinator)

UNIT TASK ASSIGNMENT SCHEDULE

This is: (check one)

_____ An initial task assignment schedule
_____ A revision of an earlier task assignment schedule

Your unit is: (circle one)

ROUTIN   COMTIN A   COMTIN B   COPE   HOPE
EMREL   CRUNODE   DECODE

Name of Assignee[a]	Task Assignments	Division of Assignment
_____	_____	_____
_____	_____	_____
_____	_____	_____
_____	_____	_____
_____	_____	_____
_____	_____	_____
_____	_____	_____
_____	_____	_____

Authorizing signature(s)[b] _____

_____

_____

_____

Acknolwedging EMREL Signature[c] _____

Assignment expense: $5 per new task assignee or reassigned person (paid to coordinator)

_____

[a]The head (manager, chair, director, editor, etc.) should fill in the names and assignments. Place a check mark beside the name of a new task assignee.
[b]Authorization of the head of the unit is needed on this form except in one case: if the head is being removed against his or her will.
[c]This signature by an EMREL official merely signifies his or her knowledge of this event, not his or her approval.

UNIT TASK ASSIGNMENT SCHEDULE

This is: (check one)

_____ An initial task assignment schedule
_____ A revision of an earlier task assignment schedule

Your unit is: (circle one)

ROUTIN   COMTIN A   COMTIN B   COPE   HOPE
          EMREL   CRUNODE   DECODE

Name of Assignee[a]	Task Assignments	Division of Assignment
_____	_____	_____
_____	_____	_____
_____	_____	_____
_____	_____	_____
_____	_____	_____
_____	_____	_____
_____	_____	_____

Authorizing signature(s)[b]   _____

_____

_____

_____

Acknolwedging EMREL Signature[c]   _____

Assignment expense: $5 per new task assignee or reassigned person (paid to coordinator)

_____

[a]The head (manager, chair, director, editor, etc.) should fill in the names and assignments. Place a check mark beside the name of a new task assignee.

[b]Authorization of the head of the unit is needed on this form except in one case: if the head is being removed against his or her will.

[c]This signature by an EMREL official merely signifies his or her knowledge of this event, not his or her approval.

UNIT TASK ASSIGNMENT SCHEDULE

This is: (check one)

_____ An initial task assignment schedule

_____ A revision of an earlier task assignment schedule

Your unit is: (circle one)

ROUTIN   COMTIN A   COMTIN B   COPE   HOPE

EMREL   CRUNODE   DECODE

Name of Assignee[a]	Task Assignments	Division of Assignment
_____	_____	_____
_____	_____	_____
_____	_____	_____
_____	_____	_____
_____	_____	_____
_____	_____	_____
_____	_____	_____

Authorizing signature(s)[b]   _____

_____

_____

_____

Acknolwedging EMREL Signature[c]   _____

Assignment expense: $5 per new task assignee or reassigned person (paid to coordinator)

_____

[a]The head (manager, chair, director, editor, etc.) should fill in the names and assignments. Place a check mark beside the name of a new task assignee.

[b]Authorization of the head of the unit is needed on this form except in one case: if the head is being removed against his or her will.

[c]This signature by an EMREL official merely signifies his or her knowledge of this event, not his or her approval.

ROUTIN TASK UNIT:
INPUT-OUTPUT FORM

Anagrams Purchased
(To be filled in by coordinator)

1. ___ ___ ___ ___ ___ ___
2. ___ ___ ___ ___ ___ ___
3. ___ ___ ___ ___ ___ ___
4. ___ ___ ___ ___ ___ ___
5. ___ ___ ___ ___ ___ ___
6. ___ ___ ___ ___ ___ ___
7. ___ ___ ___ ___ ___ ___
8. ___ ___ ___ ___ ___ ___
9. ___ ___ ___ ___ ___ ___
10. ___ ___ ___ ___ ___ ___

Words Completed
(To be filled in by task unit)

1. ___ ___ ___ ___ ___ ___
2. ___ ___ ___ ___ ___ ___
3. ___ ___ ___ ___ ___ ___
4. ___ ___ ___ ___ ___ ___
5. ___ ___ ___ ___ ___ ___
6. ___ ___ ___ ___ ___ ___
7. ___ ___ ___ ___ ___ ___
8. ___ ___ ___ ___ ___ ___
9. ___ ___ ___ ___ ___ ___
10. ___ ___ ___ ___ ___ ___

_____
(Head of purchasing unit)

Charge per order: $5 (paid to coordinator)

ROUTIN TASK UNIT:
INPUT-OUTPUT FORM

Anagrams Purchased
(To be filled in by coordinator)

1. ___ ___ ___ ___ ___ ___
2. ___ ___ ___ ___ ___ ___
3. ___ ___ ___ ___ ___ ___
4. ___ ___ ___ ___ ___ ___
5. ___ ___ ___ ___ ___ ___
6. ___ ___ ___ ___ ___ ___
7. ___ ___ ___ ___ ___ ___
8. ___ ___ ___ ___ ___ ___
9. ___ ___ ___ ___ ___ ___
10. ___ ___ ___ ___ ___ ___

Words Completed
(To be filled in by task unit)

1. ___ ___ ___ ___ ___ ___
2. ___ ___ ___ ___ ___ ___
3. ___ ___ ___ ___ ___ ___
4. ___ ___ ___ ___ ___ ___
5. ___ ___ ___ ___ ___ ___
6. ___ ___ ___ ___ ___ ___
7. ___ ___ ___ ___ ___ ___
8. ___ ___ ___ ___ ___ ___
9. ___ ___ ___ ___ ___ ___
10. ___ ___ ___ ___ ___ ___

_____
(Head of purchasing unit)

Charge per order: $5 (paid to coordinator)

WITHDRAWAL/DEPOSIT OF ASSETS FORM

Please withdraw/deposit (circle one) _____ from/to (circle one) the assets of (circle one):
(specify amount)

ROUTIN   COMTIN A   COMTIN B

_____
(Task unit head)

- -

Form I

Session #_____

WITHDRAWAL/DEPOSIT OF ASSETS FORM

Please withdraw/deposit (circle one) _____ from/to (circle one) the assets of (circle one):
(specify amount)

ROUTIN   COMTIN A   COMTIN B

_____
(Task unit head)

- -

Form I

Session #_____

WITHDRAWAL/DEPOSIT OF ASSETS FORM

Please withdraw/deposit (circle one) _____ from/to (circle one) the assets of (circle one):
(specify amount)

ROUTIN   COMTIN A   COMTIN B

_____
(Task unit head)

Organization #_____

DECODE ORGANIZATIONAL DIAGNOSIS REPORT

TO: Head of DECODE:

To facilitate discussion of the development of the total organization, please prepare one copy of this report *before* the end of each session of play. (Additional copies of Form J may be found in the manuals of other organizational members.)

Turn in your report to the coordinator *before* the end of each session.

_____

1. Identify and describe the major problems confronting the total organization during this session. Who was involved? What is the organization doing about it? What is DECODE doing about it?

_____

_____

_____

_____

_____

_____

2. Are there any conflicts in the organization at this time? If so, please describe these conflicts, including their nature, the issues involved, the primary parties, and what (if anything) is being done to resolve them.

_____

_____

_____

_____

_____

_____

3. Please describe any management systems that have been created within the organization. Where are they located? How effective are they?

_____

_____

_____

_____

_____

_____

4. Who are currently the most influential individuals in your organization? Why?

_____

_____

_____

_____

_____

_____

5. What is the most important thing that could be done right now to enhance the culture and effectiveness of your organization?

_____

_____

_____

_____

_____

_____

_____

(Head of DECODE)

Organization #_____

DECODE ORGANIZATIONAL DIAGNOSIS REPORT

TO: Head of DECODE:

To facilitate discussion of the development of the total organization, please prepare one copy of this report *before* the end of each session of play. (Additional copies of Form J may be found in the manuals of other organizational members.)

Turn in your report to the coordinator *before* the end of each session.

_____

1. Identify and describe the major problems confronting the total organization during this session. Who was involved? What is the organization doing about it? What is DECODE doing about it?

_____
_____
_____
_____
_____
_____
_____

2. Are there any conflicts in the organization at this time? If so, please describe these conflicts, including their nature, the issues involved, the primary parties, and what (if anything) is being done to resolve them.

_____
_____
_____
_____
_____
_____

3. Please describe any management systems that have been created within the organization. Where are they located? How effective are they?

_____
_____
_____
_____
_____
_____

4. Who are currently the most influential individuals in your organization? Why?

_____

_____

_____

_____

_____

_____

5. What is the most important thing that could be done right now to enhance the culture and effectiveness of your organization?

_____

_____

_____

_____

_____

_____

_____

(Head of DECODE)

COMTIN TASK UNIT:
INPUT-OUTPUT FORM

Initiating unit (circle one):   COMTIN A   COMTIN B

Puzzles Purchased   **Puzzle Solutions**
(Completed by coordinator)   (Completed by task units)

Puzzle # _____   Clue words _____ _____ _____ _____ _____
                        Answer _____

Puzzle # _____   Clue words _____ _____ _____ _____ _____
                        Answer _____

Puzzle # _____   Clue words _____ _____ _____ _____ _____
                        Answer _____

Puzzle # _____   Clue words _____ _____ _____ _____ _____
                        Answer _____

Puzzle # _____   Clue words _____ _____ _____ _____ _____
                        Answer _____

_____
(Head of initiating task unit)

Charge per order: $5 (paid to coordinator)

COMTIN TASK UNIT:
INPUT-OUTPUT FORM

Initiating unit (circle one):   COMTIN A   COMTIN B

Puzzles Purchased   **Puzzle Solutions**
(Completed by coordinator)   (Completed by task units)

Puzzle # _____   Clue words _____ _____ _____ _____ _____

Answer _____

Puzzle # _____   Clue words _____ _____ _____ _____ _____

Answer _____

Puzzle # _____   Clue words _____ _____ _____ _____ _____

Answer _____

Puzzle # _____   Clue words _____ _____ _____ _____ _____

Answer _____

Puzzle # _____   Clue words _____ _____ _____ _____ _____

Answer _____

_____
(Head of initiating task unit)

Charge per order: $5 (paid to coordinator)

COMTIN TASK UNIT:
INPUT-OUTPUT FORM

Initiating unit (circle one):   COMTIN A   COMTIN B

Puzzles Purchased
(Completed by coordinator)

Puzzle Solutions
(Completed by task units)

Puzzle # _____   Clue words _____ _____ _____ _____ _____

                  Answer _____

Puzzle # _____   Clue words _____ _____ _____ _____ _____

                  Answer _____

Puzzle # _____   Clue words _____ _____ _____ _____ _____

                  Answer _____

Puzzle # _____   Clue words _____ _____ _____ _____ _____

                  Answer _____

Puzzle # _____   Clue words _____ _____ _____ _____ _____

                  Answer _____

_____
(Head of initiating task unit)

Charge per order: $5 (paid to coordinator)

DECLARING A STRIKE

The following people wish to declare a strike: (please designate a head)

Head: _____

Members:

_____   _____

_____   _____

_____   _____

_____   _____

_____   _____

Statement of grievance(s) and whether work stoppage is involved: _____

_____

_____

_____

_____

_____

_____

_____

The members listed above are automatically under the protection of the strike. In addition, please place the following individuals under its protection:

_____   _____

_____   _____

_____   _____

Cost: $25 (paid to coordinator)

STRIKE TERMINATION FORM

The following strike members wish to terminate the strike immediately:
(deliver to coordinator)

_____

_____

_____

_____

_____

_____

_____

_____

_____

(Note: Must be signed by two-thirds of strike members to be valid.)

ASSESSMENT FORM

Name _____

1. My personal goals are: _____
_____
_____

2. How well are you doing in achieving your personal goals? Please tell why you feel this way.

3. Who are the three most influential people in the organization?

_____   _____   _____

4. Circle the units for which you have worked or are working:

NONE   ROUTIN   COMTIN A   COMTIN B   HOPE

COPE   EMREL   CRUNODE   DECODE

What are the goals of these units?

How well are they achieving their goals? Please explain why you feel this way.

5. How well is the total organization doing? (Please circle one.)

Very well   Fair   Not too well

Why do you feel this way?

6. How would you describe the culture and climate of the organization at present?

(Use other side if additional space is needed.)

ASSESSMENT FORM

Name _____

1. My personal goals are: _____

_____

_____

2. How well are you doing in achieving your personal goals? Please tell why you feel this way.

3. Who are the three most influential people in the organization?

_____   _____   _____

4. Circle the units for which you have worked or are working:

      NONE   ROUTIN   COMTIN A   COMTIN B HOPE

      COPE   EMREL   CRUNODE   DECODE

What are the goals of these units?

How well are they achieving their goals? Please explain why you feel this way.

5. How well is the total organization doing? (Please circle one.)

Very well   Fair   Not too well

Why do you feel this way?

6. How would you describe the culture and climate of the organization at present?

(Use other side if additional space is needed.)

Session # _____

DISMISSAL FORM

_____ has been dismissed from his/her task assignment in
(name of member)

_____ .
(unit name)

Reason for dismissal: _____

_____

_____

_____

_____   _____
(unit head)   (EMREL official)

Dismissal expense: $5 (payable by unit head to coordinator)

- -

Form P

Session # _____

QUIT FORM

I, _____ , do hereby quit my task assignment with
(your name)

_____ .
(unit name)

Reason for quitting: _____

_____

_____

_____

_____   _____
(your signature)   (unit head)

(Note: Coordinator should deliver this form to EMREL as soon as the information it contains has been recorded.)

Expense: none

Session # _____

DISMISSAL FORM

_____ has been dismissed from his/her task assignment in
(name of member)

_____ .
(unit name)

Reason for dismissal: _____

_____

_____

_____

_____   _____
(unit head)   (EMREL official)

Dismissal expense: $5 (payable by unit head to coordinator)

- -

Session #_____

QUIT FORM

I, _____ , do hereby quit my task assignment with
(your name)

_____ .
(unit name)

Reason for quitting: _____

_____

_____

_____

_____   _____
(your signature)   (unit head)

(Note: Coordinator should deliver this form to EMREL as soon as the information it contains has been recorded.)

Expense: none

VACATION FORM

I do hereby notify you that I will be on vacation during the next session of play.

Vacationer's signature: _____   _____
(Unit affiliation)

Acknowledging signature of EMREL official: _____

Fill out the following only if vacationer is controller or unit head:

I appoint the following person as acting unit head/controller during my vacation:

_____   _____
(Acting head/controller)   (Unit/function)

_____
(Location of unit function)

(Note: Base wage ticket for the vacation session must be sent with this form to the coordinator.)

Expense: $10 (paid to coordinator)

OI INVESTMENT FORM

We wish to invest the following amount in organizational improvement: $_____

Endorsing parties:

_____   _____
_____   _____
_____   _____
_____   _____

- -

OI INVESTMENT FORM

We wish to invest the following amount in organizational improvement: $_____

Endorsing parties:

_____   _____
_____   _____
_____   _____
_____   _____

- -

OI INVESTMENT FORM

We wish to invest the following amount in organizational improvement: $_____

Endorsing parties:

_____   _____
_____   _____
_____   _____
_____   _____

HRD INVESTMENT FORM

We wish to invest the following amount in human resource development: $ _____

Description of planned HRD activity:

_____

_____

_____

_____

Endorsing parties:

_____

_____

_____

_____

(Note: Must be signed by five of the unit heads.)

Form R2

Session #_____

HRD INVESTMENT FORM

We wish to invest the following amount in human resource development: $ _____

Description of planned HRD activity:

_____

_____

_____

_____

Endorsing parties:

_____

_____

_____

_____

(Note: Must be signed by five of the unit heads.)

HRD INVESTMENT REPORT FORM

We have implemented the following Human Resource Development plans, which we had prescribed at the time of our last HRD investment session:

- -

HRD INVESTMENT REPORT FORM

We have implemented the following Human Resource Development plans, which we had prescribed at the time of our last HRD investment session:

EMREL BASE WAGE REPORT FORM

Member's name (List alphabetically)[a]	Base wage for Session #[b]													
	1	2	3	4	5	6	7	8	9	10	11	12	13	14
EMREL official's initials (each session)														
Coordinator's initials (each session)														

[a]List *all* members of the organization.
[b]Use the following codes when filling in the column for each session: ✓ = base wage ticket provided; P = permanent base wage certificate provided. Leave a blank when no base wage was provided.

EMREL BASE WAGE REPORT FORM

Member's name (List alphabetically)[a]	Base wage for Session #[b]													
	1	2	3	4	5	6	7	8	9	10	11	12	13	14
EMREL official's initials (each session)														
Coordinator's initials (each session)														

[a]List *all* members of the organization.
[b]Use the following codes when filling in the column for each session: ✓ = base wage ticket provided; P = permanent base wage certificate provided. Leave a blank when no base wage was provided.

© *HarperCollins* Publishers

EMREL TASK ASSIGNMENT STATUS REPORT

Member's name (List alphabetically)[a]	Task assignment (if any)[b]													
	1	2	3	4	5	6	7	8	9	10	11	12	13	14
EMREL official's initials (each session)														
Coordinator's initials (each session)														

[a]List *all* members of the organization.

[b]Use the following codes in each column to indicate the initial task assignment of each member (circle the symbol for each unit head):

R	=	ROUTIN	D	=	DECODE
C/A	=	COMTIN A	E	=	EMREL
C/B	=	COMTIN B	CP	=	COPE
CR	=	CRUNODE	HP	=	HOPE

Use the following codes to indicate who are base wage or communication ticket controllers:

BW	=	base wage ticket controller
CT	=	communication ticket controller

EMREL TASK ASSIGNMENT STATUS REPORT

Member's name (List alphabetically)[a]	Task assignment (if any)[b]														
	1	2	3	4	5	6	7	8	9	10	11	12	13	14
EMREL official's initials (each session)														
Coordinator's initials (each session)														

[a]List *all* members of the organization.
[b]Use the following codes in each column to indicate the initial task assignment of each member (circle the symbol for each unit head):

R	=	ROUTIN	D	=	DECODE
C/A	=	COMTIN A	E	=	EMREL
C/B	=	COMTIN B	CP	=	COPE
CR	=	CRUNODE	HP	=	HOPE

Use the following codes to indicate who are base wage or communication ticket controllers:
BW = base wage ticket controller
CT = communication ticket controller

COPE REPORT OF FINANCIAL OPERATIONS

	Number of Org$ held at beginning of session:	Number of Org$ projected for end of session:
DECODE	$_____	$_____
CRUNODE	_____	_____
EMREL	_____	_____
HOPE	_____	_____
COPE	_____	_____
ROUTIN	_____	_____
COMTIN A	_____	_____
COMTIN B	_____	_____
Subtotal	$_____	

	Number of Org$ in asset accounts at beginning of session:	Number of Org$ in asset accounts projected for end of session:
ROUTIN	$_____	$_____
COMTIN A	_____	_____
COMTIN B	_____	_____
Subtotal	$_____	$_____
Organization total	$_____	$_____

_____
(Head of COPE)

COPE REPORT OF FINANCIAL OPERATIONS

	Number of Org$ held at beginning of session:	Number of Org$ projected for end of session:
DECODE	$_____	$_____
CRUNODE	_____	_____
EMREL	_____	_____
HOPE	_____	_____
COPE	_____	_____
ROUTIN	_____	_____
COMTIN A	_____	_____
COMTIN B	_____	_____
Subtotal	$_____	

	Number of Org$ in asset accounts at beginning of session:	Number of Org$ in asset accounts projected for end of session:
ROUTIN	$_____	$_____
COMTIN A	_____	_____
COMTIN B	_____	_____
Subtotal	$_____	$_____
Organization total	$_____	$_____

_____
(Head of COPE)

Organization #_____

CRUNODE INFORMATION REPORT

TO: Head of CRUNODE

    To provide a record of key events for discussing what happened in your organization, please prepare one copy of this report at the end of each session of play. Be sure to turn in your report to the coordinator *before* the end of each session.

_____

1. What key events occurred in the total organization during this session?

_____

_____

_____

_____

_____

_____

2. Were there any disagreements over the information that the coordinator provided to you?

_____

_____

_____

_____

_____

_____

3. What are the major concerns of the workers in the total organization?

_____

_____

_____

_____

_____

_____

4. Is the total organization achieving its goals? (Be specific.)

_____

_____

_____

_____

_____

_____

5. How well is the organization performing in terms of the four performance indicators and other important aspects, such as its climate and culture? (Be sure to specify the other aspects.)

_____

_____

_____

_____

_____

_____

_____
(Head of CRUNODE)

Organization #_____   Session #_____

CRUNODE INFORMATION REPORT

TO: Head of CRUNODE

    To provide a record of key events for discussing what happened in your organization, please prepare one copy of this report at the end of each session of play. Be sure to turn in your report to the coordinator *before* the end of each session.

_____

1. What key events occurred in the total organization during this session?

_____

_____

_____

_____

_____

_____

2. Were there any disagreements over the information that the coordinator provided to you?

_____

_____

_____

_____

_____

_____

3. What are the major concerns of the workers in the total organization?

_____

_____

_____

_____

_____

_____

4. Is the total organization achieving its goals? (Be specific.)

_____

_____

_____

_____

_____

5. How well is the organization performing in terms of the four performance indicators and other important aspects, such as its climate and culture? (Be sure to specify the other aspects.)

_____

_____

_____

_____

_____

_____

_____
(Head of CRUNODE)

JOB PROTECTION TICKET

This is to certify that _____ has purchased a job

(name)

protection ticket, which covers him or her for the remaining sessions of the simulation.

_____

(Coordinator or Assistant)

(Note: Two copies of this form must be completed: one for the individual to keep and one to be given to the person's unit head.)

Expense: $15 (paid to coordinator)

_ _

Form W

Session #_____

JOB PROTECTION TICKET

This is to certify that _____ has purchased a job

(name)

protection ticket, which covers him or her for the remaining sessions of the simulation.

_____

(Coordinator or Assistant)

(Note: Two copies of this form must be completed: one for the individual to keep and one to be given to the person's unit head.)

Expense: $15 (paid to coordinator)

SAVINGS AWARD FORM

The total number of Org$ in my envelope is $_____.

(Note: To be filed with the coordinator at the end of Session 3.)

_____
(name)

- -

SAVINGS AWARD FORM

The total number of Org$ in my envelope is $_____.

(Note: To be filed with the coordinator at the end of Session 3.)

_____
(name)

- -

SAVINGS AWARD FORM

The total number of Org$ in my envelope is $_____.

(Note: To be filed with the coordinator at the end of Session 3.)

_____
(name)

- -

SAVINGS AWARD FORM

The total number of Org$ in my envelope is $_____.

(Note: To be filed with the coordinator at the end of Session 3.)

_____
(name)